LEADER OF THE PACK

LEADER
OF THE
PACK

MARK W. ALLEN

iUniverse, Inc.
Bloomington

Leader of the Pack
The Fleet Submarine USS Batfish in World War II

iUniverse books may be ordered through booksellers or by contacting:

iUniverse
1663 Liberty Drive
Bloomington, IN 47403
www.iuniverse.com
1-800-Authors (1-800-288-4677)

ISBN: 978-1-4502-9891-9 (pbk)
ISBN: 978-1-4502-9892-6 (ebk)

Printed in the United States of America

iUniverse rev. date: 04/26/2011

To the officers and crew of *Batfish* during World War II

"The Administrative Division Commander does not have at his command the words to express suitably his admiration for the fighting spirit and skill of the commanding officer, officers and crew of the USS BATFISH for this splendid patrol in which three Jap submarines and their crews were sent to join their ancestors."

R.S. Benson
Administrative Commander, Submarine Advance Training and Relief Crew No. 2
First Endorsement of the *Batfish's* sixth patrol
March 5, 1945

Table of Contents

Acknowledgments

James Van Epps, USAAF (Ret.) for the narrative and video/pictures of the dramatic rescue of three downed aviators on *Batfish's* 7th patrol

Alan Guard, USN (Ret.), crewmember of USS *Ulvert M. Moore* (DE 442) for providing deck logs from *Moore* during the January 31 – February 1, 1945 depth charging of a Japanese submarine.

Shawn Younger of WWII Archives (wwiiarchives.net) who searched the National archives and provided copies of *Batfish* deck logs that filled in many holes that exist in the patrol reports.

Current Park Manager Rick Dennis and former Park Managers Charles and Linda Fletcher for their friendship and support over the years.

Fellow volunteers Barre McGowen and Ed Williams, two of the best "shipmates" anyone could ask to work with.

My sweet wife Leilani, for editing several drafts of this book and for accompanying me on our many trips to *Batfish* each year. I do not think she knew what she signed up for when I proposed to her in *Batfish's* conning tower that cold November afternoon.

List of Illustrations

List of Tables

Chapter 1: A Wolf in Sheep's Clothing

TOP DOG X SUB CONTACT X POSITION ABLE SIX TWO X COURSE ONE TWO OH X SPEED TWELVE X RED OR BLUE X CONFIRM X JAKE X.[1] Minutes later the other five submarines in the wolf pack responded in the negative. Lieutenant Commander Jake Fyfe knew it was a Japanese submarine. Silently closing the target on the surface, the night was dark and the enemy submarine was barely visible from *Batfish's* bridge. Seconds before firing, the Japanese submarine changed course. Had the *Batfish* been sighted? Fyfe increased speed to flank, working up ahead of the enemy's track. Fyfe maneuvered *Batfish* ahead of the Japanese submarine, finally reaching the point of attack. When Fyfe had closed to 900 yards from the target, he ordered tubes one, two and three fired. Tube one was a hot run in the tube; he immediately ordered two and then three fired. Minutes later, the torpedo from tube two hit the Japanese submarine creating a brilliant explosion, destroying the target, so much so that the third torpedo failed to detonate. *Batfish* claimed its first Japanese submarine.

On its sixth patrol, *Batfish* was in two different wolf packs. The first one was with *Archerfish* (SS 311) and *Blackfish* (SS 211) known as Joe's Jugheads with Commander Joseph E. Enright, Commanding Officer of the *Archerfish* in overall command. In mid-patrol, *Plaice* (SS 390), *Scabbardfish* (SS 397) and *Sea Poacher* (SS 406) joined the three submarines for a time before Admiral Charles Lockwood ordered them elsewhere. Lockwood deployed all six submarines in a scouting line to intercept four Japanese submarines that were involved in evacuation operations.[2] Fortunately, for *Batfish*, it was lucky enough to be in the right place at the right time to send three of the four submarines to the bottom.

The wolf pack technique, modeled after German u-boats tactics in the North Atlantic, proved effective later in World War II for U.S. submarines. This technique improved the effectiveness of submarines in three important ways. First, it increased the efficiency of the submarine as a reconnaissance craft; second, it enhanced the submarine as an attack weapon; and third, it improved the attack potential of the submarine by making feasible the night surface attack.[3] Over the next two nights, Fyfe would intercept and sink two more Japanese submarines. One day later, another submarine in the wolf pack, *Archerfish*, sank a fourth submarine. The wolves of Joe's Jugheads definitely had teeth, taking a bite out of Japanese submarine operations in February 1945, sinking four Japanese submarines in four days.

Now, fast forward 66 years and thousands of miles from the waters north of the Philippines. In the middle of the American Midwest, hundreds of miles from any ocean, is a submarine resting in a bean field.[4] *Batfish*, the top wolf of Joe's Jugheads, is now long in the tooth, stripped of armament and slowly succumbing to the elements. *Batfish* has lost her bite. The wolf is in sheep's clothing. At one time *Batfish* and hundreds of other submarines just like her prowled the Pacific, decimating Japanese commerce shipping. Today, those submarines are mostly memories, their exploits forgotten, remembered by few. *Batfish* was one of the lucky ones, becoming a museum with the intent to educate the public and honor our veterans, but mostly so others would not forget.

When you think of World War II, and in particular the Pacific Theater, what normally comes to mind? A poll produced these responses as the top ten things people envision when thinking of the Pacific conflict: aircraft carriers/battles (20.3%), atomic bombings (14.1%); island fighting, (14.1%); Pearl Harbor (12.5%), Kamikazes (7.8 %), battleships (7.8 %); submarines (6.25%); individual people (6.25%); Japanese atrocities (6.25%) and air combat (4.69%). Generally, history books attribute the American victory in the Pacific theater to air power with aircraft provided by aircraft carriers (supported by a powerful surface fleet) and land-based bombing made possible by amphibious operations (or the island-hopping campaign) in the Central Pacific. Although air power played a significant role in the defeat of Japan, this take on history minimizes the cumulative submarine attrition that did so much to bring Japan to its economic knees. However, can we really blame history books for this? After all, the submarine force was, and still is, known as the "Silent Service" with many of their exploits kept confidential for years after the war. As one example illustrating the secrecy put on submarines and their operations and tactics in World War II, commander of submarine forces in the Pacific, Admiral Charles Lockwood said:

> I told him [Secretary of the Navy, James Forrestal] briefly the stories of the recent exploits of *Barb* and *Batfish*, explaining that *Barb's* story, judiciously edited, could be told without harming submarine security, but that *Batfish's* sinking of three enemy subs was too packed with secret information to permit release. Actually, with the war drawing toward its end, I was anxious to release as much submarine publicity as could be done with safety. I felt that our lads, who were doing such a splendid job, should get a bit of recognition now and then; other wise the country, by reading the press releases, might gain the impression that the zoomies [pilots] were winning this war singlehanded.[5]

Lockwood was aware of the large number of forces fighting in the Pacific at that time, each as part of a splendid team, and he opposed the idea of anyone claiming the title "Winner of the War", but due to the nature of the Silent Service, most mission details remained classified.

Batfish was a typical fleet submarine that served in the Pacific during World War II. The submarine, its commanding officers, and crew went about their business conducting unrestricted warfare against Japanese shipping. And they did it like the other 262 submarines that also patrolled the Pacific Ocean. In the two years that *Batfish* served during World War II, it conducted seven patrols, sank sixteen ships (credited for only seven), damaged three more ships and rescued three aviators. Some submarines sank more ships; other did not sink as many. Several submarines did not sink any ships and worse yet some submarines never returned from their last patrol. In comparison, the top scoring submarines were *Tautog* (SS-199) sinking twenty-six ships on thirteen patrols, *Flasher* (SS-249) sinking 100,231 tons of shipping in six patrols, and *Tigrone* (SS-419) rescuing thirty-one downed aviators over three patrols.

From studying *Batfish's* war history, three things seemingly kept it from being higher in the list of top-scoring submarines. First, *Batfish* entered World War II two years after the war began. Some of the top scoring submarines had these two extra years to conduct additional patrols against Japanese shipping. *Batfish* departed on its first war patrol with only a little more than a year and a half left in the war, allowing it only seven patrols. Second, by the time *Batfish* made its seventh and last patrol, there simply were not any Japanese ships left to sink. Third, it seems *Batfish*, during the first two patrols, suffered from what the Navy defined as the "skipper problem".[6]

For at least a decade prior to the war, the men who became the commanding officers of submarines shared at least one common characteristic: they were superb technicians and formally trained as engineers.

> All were typically thirty-six to thirty-eight years old and were trained for a war against combat vessels and not commerce raiding. They were expected to stay at deep submergence and fire at warships on sound bearings alone. The idea of a night surface attack was unknown; the concept of an "end-around" to gain position in front of an oncoming target was only a dream. Fear of antisubmarine aircraft was instilled in the captains.[7]

If anything went wrong on the submarine, it was the captain's responsibility and he would normally take a career hit. Thus, all captains grew cautious and stayed on the bridge or in the conning tower continuously, eventually wearing out physically, emotionally and mentally. Therefore, it is no surprise that during the first year of the war, skipper performance was abysmal and the Navy replaced one-third of all captains for lack of aggressiveness or failure to sink ships. Their replacements were typically younger men, about thirty-two years old.[8]

This is exactly what happened to *Batfish*. Former crewmember Hughston Lowder gives us a glimpse of the condition of Lieutenant Commander (LCDR) Wayne R. Merrill after the second war patrol. "Captain Merrill had thinned from gaunt to emaciated, worn out from a thoroughly demoralizing war patrol." He also described him as being "in no condition to take *Batfish* on patrol." However, Merrill went to the base submarine commander and requested assignment to an area where he would find targets for his third war patrol.[9] It was not a matter of courage; it was a matter of training. A younger skipper, LCDR John K. Fyfe, replaced Merrill. Fyfe wasted little time in demonstrating his aggressiveness. During the transit to their patrol area on the submarines third patrol, he personally assured each man that he meant for them to do what they had come to do – namely, close and kill the enemy.[10]

Two things do separate *Batfish* from other submarines. First, it was a record-setting submarine in the Pacific Theater of World War II. As previously mentioned, in February 1945, the crew tracked, intercepted and sank three Japanese submarines in seventy-six hours. Many U.S. submarines sank two, but only *Batfish* had the "hat trick". In fact, only one other Allied submarine can claim to share the record with *Batfish*. The H.M.S. *Upholder* claims sinking three Italian submarines between August 1941 and March 1942.[11] Oddly enough, there is discrepancy surrounding these claims. Some sources claim the submarines sunk were U-boats, not Italian submarines. Other claims suggest a British cruiser sank the first submarine. As we will see, there is controversy surrounding the first Japanese submarine that Fyfe sank in February 1945.

The second thing that sets *Batfish* apart is that is it a museum boat. There are only a handful of these undersea warriors from World War II still with us today. Most are in coastal cities. Others are in better condition, due mostly to their location, which translates into more visitors and this in turn affects the bottom line of their museum. Some have better war records in regards to number of ships sunk or number of patrols made. *Batfish*, however, is probably more accessible to the majority of the population located in the middle of the United States, near three major interstates and a day's drive from the majority of the Midwest. Additionally, *Batfish* sits on dry ground, which some may complain about, but for others, this allows you to walk around the sub, examine the torpedo tubes, and get impressions and views from different angles. Most importantly, *Batfish* helps us reconnect to our past. George Santayana said, "Those who cannot remember the past are condemned to repeat it."[12] *Batfish* is part of our heritage. The crew was made of young men, most not much older than 20 years of age, risking their life to preserve our freedom. The ones that attend the annual reunion are humble men, quick to smile and easy to talk to. Unfortunately, each year their numbers decrease.

This book centers around three topics. First is a detailed evaluation of the famous sixth patrol. Second, is an attempt to identify the first of three Japanese submarines Fyfe sank in February 1945. Third, is the rescue story of three downed aviators, not told before in such detail. In order to tell this story, we must understand how *Batfish* came to be. From keel laying to commissioning *Batfish* evolved from a design on blueprints to a lethal undersea warrior. To understand how *Batfish* did its job, we need to know how it worked. Therefore, the second chapter will briefly discuss *Batfish's* commissioning, construction and layout in addition to a general overview of the submarine war against Japan. This will set the stage for Chapter 3 "On the Hunt", which provides an overview of *Batfish's* role in the Pacific War, summarizing each of the seven war patrols followed by a table of torpedo attack data.

The next two chapters go hand-in-hand. In Chapter Four "The Hunter Hunted", we examine the concept of submarines as anti-submarine warfare (ASW) weapons using *Batfish's* sixth war patrol as an example where Fyfe set a record sinking three Imperial Japanese Navy submarines in a seventy-six hour time span. Chapter Five "Mistaken Identity" discusses issues surrounding the actual identity of the first of the three Japanese submarines Fyfe sank in February 1945. There are many variations on the actual events on February 10. Some authors claim the Japanese submarine was *RO-55*, other's claim it was *RO-115*, another says it was a premature explosion of a previously fired torpedo. The official candidate is *I-41*. With only four submarines assigned to an evacuation detail, and with three of the four accounted for, can the process of elimination deduce the actual victim? All candidates are considered and evidence will reveal the most likely submarine lost to *Batfish's* second torpedo attack.

Chapter Six "Salvation" is a detailed account of *Batfish's* rescue of three aviators forced to ditch their B-25 Mitchell bomber. Previous books have only touched on the details, but personal communication with the last surviving member of the aircrew has shed some additional light on the subject. In addition, a few other documents found during internet searches contributed to a more detailed account of the only rescue *Batfish* made.

The book concludes with an overview of the submarines decommissioning after World War II, the second commissioning in the 1950's as a training vessel designated AGSS-310, and a brief discussion of the nuclear *Batfish* (SSN-681) and how it too had its own submarine vs. submarine adventure. Was it coincidence or destiny that SS310's namesake would carry on the tradition of anti-submarine warfare? Finally, we will see how *Batfish* still serves today as a museum boat in Muskogee, Oklahoma.

Chapter 2: Commissioning and the Submarine War Against Japan

During the planning stages, the Navy named her *Acoupa*. On September 24, 1942, prior to her keel laying on December 27, 1942, she was renamed *Batfish* after "any of several fishes; a pediculate fish of the West Indies, the flying gurnard of the Atlantic, or a California sting ray."[1] Although the physical comparison was unflattering, the implication of the expected performance came through loud and clear.

On December 7, 1941, the Japanese surprise attack on the U.S. fleet at Pearl Harbor brought about two significant changes on how America would fight the war in the Pacific. First, the attack left the aircraft carrier as the major offensive weapon of surface fleet, replacing the battleship. Second, the role of the submarine switched from surface fleet scout to independent commerce raider.[2] The Navy designed fleet submarines with the speed, endurance and weapon load to make them suited for attacking Japanese shipping throughout the Pacific. After Pearl Harbor, the Navy immediately assigned submarines to their new role as commerce raiders with the goal of stopping the import of raw materials to, and the export of war materials from, Japan. Japanese shipping routes spanned the Pacific and this ocean traffic was the lifeblood of Japan's war effort. Japan had few natural resources and was dependent upon imports of oil, coal, iron, food and other materials.[3] American submarines acted for the most part alone during the first two years of the war. In 1943, other American elements contributed to the destruction of the Japanese merchant fleet; however, submarines deserve most of the credit (Table 2.1).

Table 2.1 Japanese Merchant Tonnage Sunk[4]				
	# of Ships	% of Total	Tons	% of Total
Submarines	1,152.5	45.5	4,861,300	54.64
Navy Carrier Air	393.5	15.5	1,452,900	16.33
Army Air	143.5	5.7	910,100	10.23
Navy Land-Based Air	300.0	11.8	383,200	4.31
All Other Causes	543.5	21.5	1,289,500	14.49
Total	**2,533.0**	**100.0**	**8,897,000**	**100.00**

In addition to merchant ships, American submarines sank the following Japanese combatant ships: four aircraft carriers, four escort aircraft carriers, one battleship, four heavy cruisers, nine light cruisers, thirty-eight destroyers and twenty-three submarines. The total confirmed and probable Japanese naval and merchant ships sunk by submarines were 1,392 ships for 5,583,400 tons. This equated to 54.6% of all Japanese ships sunk during World War II.[5]

A maximum of 288 submarines were in the U.S. Fleet; 263 of these were operating in the Pacific during the World War II. U.S. submarines stationed in the Pacific made 1,474 war patrols, attacking 4,112 Japanese ships, claiming 1,392 ships sunk. In addition, eighty-six different submarines rescued 504 downed aviators. On the flip side, there were fifty-two submarines lost (all causes) which equated to one out of every five or 20%. In terms of personnel losses, the total was 350 officers and 3,194 enlisted personnel totaling 3,544 lost.[6]

The U.S. Pacific Submarine campaign had three major accomplishments. First, merchant marine losses crippled Japanese industry, hindering the generation of military power. Second, the destruction of both the Japanese merchant marine and Imperial Japanese Navy's capital ships severely limited Japan's ability to project power throughout the Pacific. Third, the use of the submarine enabled the U.S. Navy to take offensive actions in Japanese-controlled waters and inflict disproportionate losses relative to the U.S. investment in submarines.[7]

A submarines primary mission in World War II was the execution of successful torpedo attacks against Japanese shipping. The types of targets a submarine encountered ranged from single merchantmen, to convoys, and task forces. Destroyers, destroyer escorts, patrol crafts or sometimes aircraft normally escorted these vessels. The delivery of these torpedoes, called the approach and attack, required the submarine to gain a favorable firing position, usually ahead of the target.

The process of approaching and attacking a target involves three phases; the contact phase, the approach phase, and the attack phase. The purpose of the contact phase is to determine the direction of relative movement of the target. Once the contact bearing and course is established, the contact phase is completed and the approach phase begins. The purpose of the approach phase is to get closer to the target in order to bring the submarine within torpedo range. The submerged submarine's greatest problem is to gain a good position from which to deliver the attack. The best position is directly ahead of the target at a range that will allow time for the submarine to maneuver to a favorable firing position. Once the submarine is ahead of the target and starts to maneuver into a favorable firing position, the approach phase is over and the attack phase begins. The purpose of the attack phase is to maneuver the submarine into the most favorable firing position obtainable under the circumstances. Each *Batfish* attack described in Chapter 3 uses terminology such as starboard track, gyro angle, track angle and so forth. These terms are defined in the Glossary section near the end of the book. In addition, Figure 2.1 provides a visual understanding of terms.

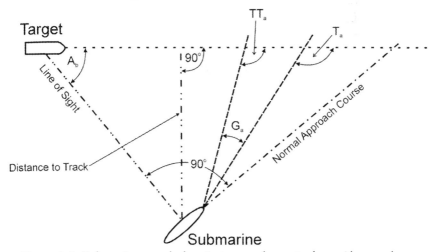

Figure 2.1. Submarine attack descriptions and terminology. Ab = angle on bow, TTa = torpedo track angle, Ta = track angle, Ga = gyro angle.

Batfish is a Balao-class submarine, also known as a "thick-skinned" boat due to a thicker pressure hull than their predecessors of the Gato-class submarines. Gato-class submarines have a pressure hull made of mild steel, 11/16 inches thick whereas the Balao-class submarines have high-tensile steel pressure hulls approximately 7/8 inches thick.[8] The thicker pressure hull of the Balao-class allowed the submarine to dive deeper, with a 400-foot operating depth (as opposed to a 300-foot operating depth for the Gato class) and a 675-foot "collapse depth".[9] *Batfish* is also a diesel-electric boat, using four Fairbanks-Morse diesel engines while on the surface and four General Electric motors while submerged to propel the submarine through the water. Batteries powered the sub while submerged and would drain quickly if the crew did not conserve power. Submarines would surface, most commonly at night, and use one or more engines to charge the batteries. The Balao-class submarine usually had a crew of eighty to eighty-five men, ten of which were officers. Table 2.2 lists some basic specifications for a Balao-class submarine.

Batfish is divided into several compartments.[10] Each compartment usually has several uses. Beginning at the forward end, the compartments are: forward torpedo room, forward battery, control room, crews mess, aft battery and crews quarters, forward engine room, aft engine room, maneuvering room, and aft torpedo room. The forward torpedo room carried sixteen of the twenty-four torpedoes taken on a patrol. Crewmembers slept on bunks above and attached to the torpedo loading skids. The forward battery consists of two decks. The lower deck contained 126 battery cells that powered the submarine when submerged. The upper deck contained officer sleeping quarters, the officer's wardroom and the yeoman's office.

Aft of the forward battery is the control room that is the nerve center of the submarine. On the main deck is the helm, diving station and radio room. Below the main deck is the pump room. Above the control room is the conning tower that contains the periscopes, sonar, radar, torpedo data computer (TDC) and firing controls. A hatch in the conning tower leads up to the bridge. The next section aft of the control room is the galley, the crew's mess and berthing for almost half of the crew. On the lower deck is the aft battery that contained another set of battery cells, along with cold storage and the gun locker. The forward and aft engine rooms each house two Fairbanks-Morse diesel engines that span both decks. A watertight door separates each compartment.

Aft of the engine rooms is the maneuvering room. Occupying the majority of this room is the main propulsion control cubicle. The cubicle routed electricity from each of the four generators and storage batteries to connections for the main propulsion motors that are located on the lower deck of the maneuvering room. The cubicle could connect one or more generators to the batteries for charging. Through a watertight door on the aft bulkhead of the maneuvering room is the aft torpedo room. Similar to the forward torpedo room, this room has four tubes and would normally contain eight torpedoes. In addition, there was berthing for nearly twenty-four men.

Table 2.2 Specifications for a Balao-Class Submarine[11]	
Length	311 ft., 9 in.
Beam	27 ft., 3 in.
Draft	15 ft., 3 in.
Surfaced Displacement	1,525 tons
Submerged Displacement	2,415 tons
Complement	10 Officers / 70-75 Crew
Surface Plant	4 – 1,350 BHP Fairbanks-Morse Diesel Engines
Submerged Plant	4 – 685 HP General Electric Motors
Batteries	2 sets of 126 Exide Storage Cells
Surface Speed	20.25 knots
Surface Endurance	10,000 miles at 10 knots
Submerged Speed	8.75 knots
Submerged Endurance	48 hours at 2 knots
Test Depth	400 feet
Estimated Collapse Depth	675 feet
Tubes: bow	6 X 21 inch
Tubes: aft	4 X 21 inch
Torpedoes	24 (16 forward, 8 aft)

Fleet submarines such as *Batfish* had a patrol endurance of approximately eight weeks with most patrols ranging from forty-two to fifty-six days; the limiting factor was normally weapon or fuel considerations. The typical fleet submarine, with six 21-inch torpedo tubes forward and four tubes in the aft torpedo room, usually carried a maximum of twenty-four Mark-14 or Mark-23 steam, or Mark-18 electric torpedoes. Sometimes submarines carried a mixed load of steam and electric torpedoes and on rare occasions, some submarines carried mines in place of some of their normal torpedo load.

Batfish, constructed at the Portsmouth Naval Shipyard in New Hampshire, was launched May 5, 1943 under the sponsorship of Mrs. Nellie W. Fortier, and commissioned on August 21, 1943. Upon commissioning, Lieutenant Commander Wayne R. Merrill, USN, assumed command of *Batfish*. The United States flag flew above the *Batfish's* stern as the crew stood rigidly proud in salute. Then Merrill read his orders. Shakedown training began the next day.

Merrill held post-commissioning shakedown exercises around Portsmouth, New Hampshire. During the month of training exercises included in the shakedown cruise, about 66% of the crew required qualification in, and also to learn the war time procedure of, submarines. Merrill held daily diving, gunnery and seamanship drills. In mid-September, *Batfish* sailed for Newport, Rhode Island for torpedo exercises and then on to New London, Connecticut, arriving on September 26, where gunnery drills took priority. While in New London, *Batfish* had to pass the rigid operational readiness inspection to prove to the Commander of Submarines Atlantic that the submarine was ready to go to war. On October 9, *Batfish* passed her exams and went back to New London for minor repairs, fuel, provisions, and a full load of live ammunition.

On October 14, *Batfish* embarked towards Pearl Harbor via the Panama Canal after the Navy pronounced the submarine ready for battle. On November 8, *Batfish* entered the Bay of Panama and began the journey westward across the Pacific to Pearl Harbor. On November 19, *Batfish* reached the rendezvous point off Oahu and *YMS 286* escorted the submarine into Pearl Harbor.

On December 11, 1941, the American submarine, *Gudgeon* (SS 211), departed Pearl Harbor, becoming the first U.S. submarine to undertake an "Empire" patrol.[12] Two years later to the day, at 1 p.m. on December 11, 1943, *Batfish* backed from the dock, departing on her first war patrol. The submarine and her crew were now at war with Japan.

Chapter 3: On the Hunt

Batfish made seven war patrols during World War II. The average war patrol lasted approximately two months with about a two-week break between patrols as the submarine was back at one of the bases being re-supplied, having new equipment installed and fixing any damage sustained.

Batfish, in seven war patrols, claimed sixteen ships sunk for 41,384 tons, and damaged three other ships (Table 3.1). The Joint Army-Navy Assessment Committee (JANAC) officially credited *Batfish* with only seven ships, for 11,810 tons.[1] This accreditation is par for the statistical course. Generally, JANAC credited American submarines with only half of what they sank - or claimed twice as many ships as were later substantiated.

Table 3.1. War Patrol Results - Summary							
Patrol #	Torpedoes Fired	Hits	Sunk (Patrols)	Sunk (Official)	Tonnage (Patrols)	Tonnage (Official)	Ships Damaged
1	8	5	2	1	15,678	5,486	None
2	0	0	0	0	0	0	None
3	16	4	5	1	9,206	990	None
4	9	5	2	2	2,700	2,072	None
5	21	5	4	0	9,300	0	2 - 4,300
6	17	5	3	3	4,500	3,262	1 - 200
7	0	0	0	0	0	0	None
Totals	**71**	**24**	**16**	**7**	**41,384**	**11,810**	**3 - 4,500**

Taken solely from the patrol reports, this chapter briefly summarizes each patrol and describes each torpedo and gun attack in the order they happened. Descriptions include general statistics and information regarding the Japanese ships attacked. For a more in-depth description of each patrol, please visit the patrol reports list on the *Batfish* website. Figure 3 illustrates patrol areas for all seven patrols.

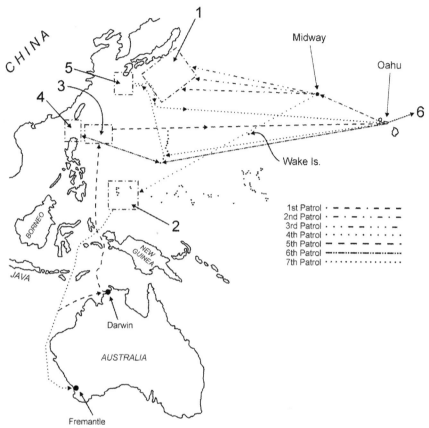

Figure 3.1. *Batfish* patrol areas. 1=patrols one, two and three, 2=patrol four, 3=patrol five, 4=patrol six, 5=patrol seven, 6=to San Francisco between patrols six and seven.

War Patrol #1

Batfish's first patrol was from December 11, 1943 to January 31, 1944 with a patrol area south of Honshu, Japan. Merrill was in command and fired eight torpedoes, hitting with five of them reporting two ships sunk for 15,678 tons. However, the official total was only one ship for 5,486 tons. The Navy designated this patrol as successful for the Combat Insignia Award.

Patrol No. 1.
Torpedo Attack No. 1
Date: 1-20-44. Time: 0057(I)
Lat: 31-30N, Long: 134-51E

Merrill attacked and damaged a passenger-freighter similar to the *Ginyo Maru* at 8,613 tons. The target was one of four ships in a convoy escorted by one corvette and one trawler-type patrol vessel. During daylight, this convoy also had air escort of at least one Japanese Navy single float biplane. A periscope sweep sighted smoke from two of the ships as Merrill conducted a submerged patrol. Visibility was good with scattered clouds, but Merrill was unable to get close enough to the convoy for a submerged attack. Surfacing at dusk, Merrill chased the convoy, using radar to regain contact. At the time of attack, the night was very clear and dark with starlight giving excellent visibility. Merrill attacked the on the surface just ten minutes before moonrise. The target was on course 325° with a speed of nine knots and at a range of 3,400 yards and was in fairly light condition (i.e. apparently not carrying any cargo) with a draft of ten feet (loaded was about twenty-eight feet). *Batfish* was on the surface and matching the speed of nine knots on course 030°.

Merrill performed a surfaced radar attack using visual bearings from the target bearing transmitter (TBT). The tracking party obtained course and speed and verified by the TDC. Merrill continually pointed the submarine's bow at the target until just prior to firing at which point the submarine steadied on a given course, thereby minimizing the submarine's silhouette. The firing range was greater than desired, but was necessary due to the occasional rapid closing of the escort that at times headed directly at *Batfish*. Merrill believed this was a coincidence and credited the submarines new camouflage in keeping *Batfish* virtually invisible at night.

The torpedoes were set to run at a depth of ten feet due to the light draft of the target and the fact that a moderate sea was running. Merrill selected tubes deepest in the water because it was a surface attack (Table 3.2). Merrill fired three torpedoes eight to ten seconds apart using a spread of 0°, 1° left, 1° right; there were no indications of erratic performance as all torpedoes ran hot, straight and normal. The first torpedo hit the target. Those on *Batfish*'s bridge witnessed an explosion at the water line and felt as well as heard the impact. The target stopped dead in water, took a list to port, and settled by the stern. It then began a frantic signal to the escort for help. The second torpedo missed ahead due to the size of spread used, the third torpedo passed astern, hitting another ship in the convoy which would be the target ship of Attack #2 a few seconds later. JANAC listed this ship as the 5,486-ton *Hidaka Maru* that Merrill attacked a second time, described below in Attack #3.

Patrol No. 1.
Torpedo Attack No. 2
Date: 1-20-44. Time: 0058(I)
Lat: 31-30N, Long: 134-51E

Merrill attacked and sank a ship similar to the 7,065-ton *Tatukami Maru*. The attack on the *Tatukami Maru*, also part of the four-ship convoy, commenced eighteen seconds after completion of Attack #1. The target was heavily loaded with a draft of 26½ feet (light draft would be around 9½ feet) and was on a base course of 325° with a speed of nine knots and at a range of 3,600 yards. *Batfish* was still on the surface, heading 030° at nine knots.

Merrill fired three upper bow tubes using a spread of 0°, 1° left, and 1° right (Table 3.2). Three torpedoes hit this target: the third torpedo fired in Attack #1 and the first and second torpedoes from this attack. The third torpedo from this attack missed astern, due to the size of the torpedo spread versus the range to target.

Sound heard the explosions of three torpedoes, hitting at times corresponding to the calculated torpedo runs. A cloud of black smoke enveloped the target and, at the same time, it disappeared from the radar screen. Sound picked up many loud crackling noises. Although partially obscured by smoke, *Tatukami Maru* definitely sank, verified a few minutes later as efforts to find the ship in the vicinity of the attack proved fruitless. JANAC gave no official credit for this sinking.

Patrol No. 1.
Torpedo Attack No. 3
Date: 1-20-44. Time: 0509(I)
Lat: 31-28N, Long: 134-52E

The target was the *Hidaka Maru*, the same ship damaged in Attack #1. Merrill knew the approximate location of the *Hidaka Maru* from the previous attack and contact was quickly regained using radar. With very bright moonlight providing excellent visibility, lookouts sighted the target from the bridge at a range of 14,000 yards and Merrill attacked this ship a second time. *Batfish* was on the surface, heading 020° at nine knots. Using radar ranges and visual bearings, *Hidaka Maru* was dead in the water, stopped and drifting on heading 100° and at a range of 6,000 yards. The target draft was about thirty feet aft and five feet forward. A corvette type escort was circling it at about 1,500 to 2,500 yards but not adhering to a fixed patrol pattern.

Merrill attacked using a combination of visual bearings and radar making it necessary to approach the target with the moon nearly astern in order to gain a position on the target's beam. There was insufficient time before daylight to get on the opposite side of the target, so Merrill decided to fire low-power shots at a considerable range. *Batfish* was conned from the bridge to approach on a 100° starboard track. Merrill fired torpedoes from tubes five and six using 0° gyro angles with ten-foot depth settings (Table 3.2). The first torpedo hit just abaft starboard beam throwing up a geyser of water and white smoke. The second torpedo probably passed under the bow, which had raised clear of the water, and did not detonate. The ship took an increased port list and began to settle by the stern until water was above the main deck level and open air showed under the bow for a distance of fifty to seventy-five feet abaft the stern. Seven minutes after the torpedo hit there was a loud, under water explosion audible for miles. The radar pip separated into two smaller pips at this time and only the forward part of the superstructure and the bow were visible above water. Coming daylight prevented watching *Hidaka Maru* from completely sinking, however, JANAC credited *Batfish* with this sinking.

Table 3.2 War Patrol #1 Torpedo Summary						
Attack 1						
Tube	Track	Gyro	Depth	Hit/Miss	Erratic	Type
4	129° P	346°	10'	Hit	No	14-3A
5	131° P	344°	10'	Miss	No	14-3A
6	129½° P	345½°	10'	Hit[a]	No	14-3A
Attack 2						
1	128° P	347°	10'	Hit	No	14-3A
2	130° P	345°	10'	Hit	No	14-3A
3	128° P	347°	10'	Miss	No	14-3A
Attack 3						
5	100° S	0°	10'	Hit	No	14-3A
6	100° S	0°	10'	Miss	No	14-3A

a: hit on another ship (same ship as Attack 2)

War Patrol #2

Batfish's second patrol was from February 22 to April 15, 1944 patrolling the area off the southeast coast of Shikoku. The Navy designated this patrol as not successful for the Combat Insignia Award as Merrill did not perform any attacks or fire any torpedoes. Merrill summarized the patrol:

> "In the opinion of the Commanding Officer the lack of success on this patrol must been attributed to the nearly complete absence of enemy traffic through the area. At no time were there any indications of merchant shipping having passed through the area. On four occasions attempts were made to intercept men-of-war, none of which were successful. In two of these instances the targets were submarines. It is believed that deviations from the supposed tracks, or schedules, caused failure of the other two attempts on surface craft. In spite of difficulties due to weather, our navigational position was pretty accurately determined in each case."[2]

War Patrol #3

Batfish's third patrol was from May 26 to July 7, 1944 patrolling the area from Honshu southwestward to Kyushu. LCDR John K. Fyfe replaced Merrill as skipper of *Batfish*. Fyfe fired sixteen torpedoes, hitting with four of them and sank five ships totaling 9,206 tons; however, the official total was only one ship for 990 tons. The Navy designated this patrol as successful for the Combat Insignia Award.

Patrol No. 3
Torpedo Attack No. 1
Date: 10 June. Time: 1243(I)
Lat: 32-38N, Long: 131-58E

Fyfe picked up the target close inshore and then attacked and sank a 3,000-3,500 ton MFM (mast-funnel-mast) training ship based on the number of men who were drilling topside. What appeared to be a training ship had two guns forward, at least one aft, and a draft of about ten feet.

She was cruising on various courses but seemed to be following no zigzag plan and did not seem to be heading for any place in particular. At the time of attack, the target was on course 110° with a speed of 7.5 knots and at a range of 1,970 yards. *Batfish* was at periscope depth and traveling at two knots on course 220°.

Fyfe fired tubes one, two and three on a 70° port track using a 1° divergent spread with a distance to target of 1,900 yards. The torpedoes were set for six feet (Table 3.3). The sea was glassy but visibility was only fair. About fifteen seconds before the first torpedo hit, the crew on the ship apparently saw the torpedo wakes and the ship started to turn toward, or into, the wakes to try to comb them. The first torpedo hit after a run of one minute and thirty-three seconds; the second and third torpedoes missed. The first torpedo struck the ship amidships and the ship literally fell apart and sank very quickly. The torpedo explosion was exceptionally loud, followed three minutes later by another explosion, probably a magazine or a boiler blowing up. JANAC did not award official credit for this ship.

Patrol No. 3
Torpedo Attack No. 2
Date: 18 June. Time: 1328(I)
Lat: 33-26N, Long: 135-34E

Fyfe attacked and sank a coastal MFM cargo ship, with two three-inch guns, similar to the 2,232-ton *Mayati Maru*. The *Mayati Maru* sailed with a small coastal tanker and at first Fyfe thought it was an escort for the tanker. At the time of the attack, the target had a draft of nine feet, was traveling at eight knots on course 275° and was at a range of 2,130 yards. *Batfish* was at periscope depth, traveling at 2.5 knots on course 325°.

Fyfe planned to get both ships with a spread of three torpedoes. The targets were on a westerly course close to shore off Shiono Misaki and at the time of firing the cargo ship was to seaward and abeam of the tanker. Fyfe fired torpedoes from tubes one, two and three on a 120° port track using a 2° divergent spread at a range of 2,100 yards (Table 3. 3). The point of aim was the overlap between the targets that was 1/3 of the target length inside the stern of the cargo ship and the bow of the tanker. The second torpedo hit just aft of the bridge after a one minute and thirty second run. The first and third torpedoes missed astern. Fyfe saw the target break in half and sink stern first in less than a minute. JANAC did not award official credit for this ship.

Patrol No. 3
Torpedo Attack No. 3
Date: 22 June. Time: 1212(I)
Lat: 34-35N, Long: 137-56E

Fyfe attacked an engines-aft coastal cargo ship proceeding on an easterly course close inshore. She was somewhat similar to the 3,110 ton *Anastasia* except that she had two heavy large masts, two cranes, a high bow and a design and simplicity that was conducive to mass production. The target had a draft of 15 feet, was traveling at four knots on a course of 095° and was at a range of 1,900 yards. *Batfish* was at periscope depth, on course 025° with a speed of 2.5 knots.

Fyfe launched a periscope attack after a long approach at high speed. Fyfe fired three torpedoes from the bow tubes using a 1° divergent spread, 90° starboard track, 1900 yards range. All torpedoes missed astern (Table 3. 3). The range was actually 3,800 yards instead of 1,900 so Fyfe started a new approach. Just before firing a second time at this target, the ship turned away 40°. Thinking that the target had seen the torpedo wakes, Fyfe took a sweep with the periscope and saw another cargo ship approaching on an opposite course from the first ship. Therefore, Fyfe checked his fire and swung the submarine for an attack (Attack #4) on the approaching ship that was to seaward of the submarine.

Patrol No. 3
Torpedo Attack No. 4
Date: 22 June. Time: 1255(I)
Lat: 34-35N, Long: 137-51E

Fyfe attacked and sank the 3,110 ton *Anastasia*, a modern coastal cargo ship with a draft of fifteen feet, and a sister ship of that described under Attack #3. Following the previous attack, Fyfe sighted this target on the starboard quarter at a range of 5,000 yards. When attacked, the ship was on a westerly course of 273°, a speed of 4.5 knots and a range of 1,700 yards. *Batfish* was still at periscope depth and maintained its 2.5-knot speed, but Fyfe changed course to 005°.

Fyfe setup on this new ship and fired four torpedoes from the stern tubes on a 95° starboard track using a 2° divergent spread (Table 3. 3). Fyfe saw two torpedoes hit the target, timed as first and third torpedoes. The first hit was just forward of the engine room and the second just inside the bow. The ship sank stern first with a large starboard list. JANAC officially credited *Batfish* with sinking the 990-ton *Nagaragwa Maru*.

Patrol No. 3
Torpedo Attack No. 5
Date: 29 June. Time: 2316(I)
Lat: 34-08N, Long: 139-49E

On this attack, SJ radar picked up a surface contact on bearing 276° at a range of 12,100 yards. The plot began tracking the target while Fyfe performed an end around. Almost two hours later, *Batfish* was ahead of the contact and in position to begin an attack. Originally, Fyfe thought the target was a tanker but eventually believed it was an LST (with an estimated draft of four feet) escorted by two high-speed anti-submarine vessels of unknown type. The convoy was changing course between 335° and 015° on four, five and seven minute legs with an estimated speed of thirteen knots.

Fyfe had *Batfish* moving at 2.5 knots on course 396°. After a long end around chase, Fyfe dove to radar depth when he achieved the desired position ahead of the convoy. With the target at a range of 3,350 yards, Fyfe, using periscope bearings and radar ranges, fired three bow tubes on a 116° starboard track, with a 1° divergent spread and torpedoes set to run at six feet (Table 3. 3). No hits. From an analysis of the problem and from the information received from sound, these torpedoes passed underneath the target. Sound tracked the torpedoes to the target but lost them in the target's wake shortly thereafter. The TDC set up generated ranges and bearings that required no correcting over a period of nearly six minutes, just prior to and after firing. The target started signaling to the escort with a red blinker gun at the time the torpedoes should have reached the target's track. The torpedoes ran directly down a moon slick so it is doubtful the target saw the wakes in time to avoid. The only explanation that Fyfe could give for not hitting was that he fired at an LST and the torpedoes ran underneath. The target through the periscope appeared only as a blob with no distinguishable features except the fact that she was low and rather long, characteristics of a tanker.

Patrol No. 3
Gun Attack No. 1
Date: 1 July. Time: 1125-1300(I)
Lat: 31-45N, Long: 140-39E

Fyfe attacked and sank two ships on this patrol during surface gun action on July 1. Combined fire from the four-inch deck gun and the 20-mm gun sank the 226-ton *Isuzugawa Maru #5* and the 138-ton *Kamoi* (or *Kamo) Maru*. The four-inch gun crew fired fifty-nine rounds of high-capacity and twenty-four rounds of common shells at an average range of about 1,100 yards using radar ranges and radar spotting on the splashes. Fyfe estimated that at least 40% of the shells hit the targets. The 20-mm gun crew fired 940 rounds of high explosive incendiary and 469 rounds of high explosive tracer. The forward 20-mm jammed after the first burst and was out of action during most of the engagement. Ranges varied between 1,500 and 100 yards.

The *Isuzugawa Maru* displayed a Japanese name and seal painted on the side but no one could interpret the writing. The ship had a high bow, very high foremast with the bridge amidships, a diesel stack, raised living quarters aft and a high mainmast. Crates and drums were stowed on deck. The *Isuzugawa Maru* had three machine guns and carried three depth charges. The crew witnessed both targets sinking but the two ships did not count towards the overall total tonnage because JANAC did not apply tonnage from any merchant vessel less than 500 gross tons.[3]

Table 3.3 War Patrol #3 Torpedo Summary						
Attack 1						
Tube	Track	Gyro	Depth	Hit/Miss	Erratic	Type
1	70° P	001° 30'	6'	Hit	Normal	Mk. 23
2	70° P	359° 20'	6'	Miss	Normal	Mk. 23
3	70° P	000° 30'	6'	Miss	Normal	Mk. 23
Attack 2						
1	120° P	008°	6'	Miss	----	14-3A
2	122° P	005° 30'	6'	Hit	----	Mk. 23
3	123° P	005° 40'	6'	Miss	----	14-3A

		Attack 3					
4	90° S	005° L	6'	Miss	----	Mk. 23
5	90° S	004° 40' L	6'	Miss	----	Mk. 23
6	90° S	006° L	6'	Miss	----	Mk. 23
		Attack 4					
7	92° S	1° 00' R	6'	Hit	----	Mk. 23
8	95° S	3° 30' R	6'	Miss	----	Mk. 23
9	98° S	8° 00' R	6'	Hit	----	Mk. 23
10	100° S	5° 40' R	6'	Miss	----	14-3A
		Attack 5					
1	116° S	6° 50'L	6'	Miss	Normal	Mk. 23
2	116° S	4° 20'L	6'	Miss	Normal	14-3A
3	118° S	5° 30'L	6'	Miss	Normal	Mk. 23

War Patrol #4

Batfish's fourth patrol was from July 31 to September 12, 1944 with its patrol area around the Ngaruangl Passage - Palau Island Group. The Navy designated this patrol as successful for the Combat Insignia Award where Fyfe fired nine torpedoes, hitting with five of them. Fyfe sank two ships for 2,700 tons; however, JANAC officially credited two ships for 2,072 tons.

Patrol No. 4
Torpedo Attack No. 1
Date: 23 August. Time: 1402
Lat. 8-09N, Long: 134-38E

Fyfe attacked and sank a 1,200-ton *Minekaze* class destroyer. The destroyer was either anchored or underway and stopped, apparently standing by two beached ships: another destroyer and a small cargo ship. At the time of the attack, the target had a draft of 9.5 feet and stopped on course 143°. *Batfish* was at periscope depth, traveling at 2.5 knots on course 271°.

After Fyfe maneuvered into firing position, he fired three torpedoes from tubes one, two, and three on a 53° port track at range of 2,670 yards at the destroyer dead in the water. Fyfe aimed the torpedoes, set to run at five feet in a calm sea with no wind, at the bow, middle of target (MOT) and the stern by periscope (Table 3.4). The torpedoes smoked prohibitively all the way down the range. A few minutes later, Fyfe observed three hits: forward, aft, and amidships. The target developed a list to port and sank to bridge level a minute later. On the next observation, approximately forty-five minutes later, the ship had disappeared. JANAC officially credited this ship as the 492-ton Minesweeper *W 22*.

Patrol No. 4
Torpedo Attack No. 2
Date: 25 August. Time: 1300
Lat. 7-25N, Long: 134-31E

Fyfe attacked was a large PC type patrol vessel, first sighted at a range of 3,500 yards on a southerly course at a speed of twelve knots. *Batfish* was at periscope depth, moving at 2.5 knots on course 100°.

Plot determined the target was on course 180°, and was at a range of 1,200 to 1,300 yards. Fyfe fired torpedoes from tubes seven, eight, and nine, set to run at three feet, on a 140° port track, range 1,250 yards using a 3° spread (Table 3.4). All three missed. Fyfe believed the torpedoes broached and ran erratic. The torpedoes had 40° left gyro angles and Fyfe watched the target and not the direction in which the torpedoes ran. Sound tracked the torpedoes but the actual course was lost in the shuffle. Sea conditions were number three and visibility was about 8,000 yards.

Shortly after firing, the target turned sharply to left and then stopped. Fyfe obtained another set up on the new course and fired tube number ten on a 68° starboard track, range 1,900 yards. The torpedo was set to run at four feet. As Fyfe fired the torpedo, the target's screws started up and he swung toward *Batfish* on course 030°, increasing his speed to 4.5 knots. Sound tracked this last torpedo as running hot straight and normal but missed astern of the target.

Patrol No. 4
Torpedo Attack No. 3
Date: 26 August. Time: 1830
Lat. 8-30N, Long: 134-37E

Fyfe attacked and sank the 1,580-ton *Shiratsuyu*-class destroyer *Samidare*. The target had an estimated draft of almost ten feet. *Samidare*, grounded on Ngaruangl Reef, and was oriented at 105°. *Batfish* was at periscope depth, moving at 2.5 knots on course 207°.

Fyfe performed a periscope attack at dusk on the beached destroyer. With the range to target at 2,970 yards, Fyfe fired two Mark-18 torpedoes from tubes seven and eight, set to run at three and four feet respectively (Table 3.4). The sea was calm but had long, low ground swells. Visibility was fair with a completely overcast sky. The first torpedo partially broached three times but hit the target just aft of the #2 stack on a 101° starboard track. The second torpedo broached once, but ran straight and hit the target in practically the same place. The two confirmed hits from the Mark-18 torpedoes destroyed the target, breaking the ship in half just aft of the #2 stack and practically shearing the stern off. The foremast broke about halfway up, #2 stack bent over like a limp rag, debris and smoke flew two hundred feet in the air. The bow stayed on the reef however looking strangely desolate all by itself. Fyfe considered the target unsalvageable so he decided not to fire another torpedo. Five days later, the Japanese blew up what remained of the wreckage. JANAC credited *Batfish* with sinking this ship; however, some sources give the submarine half-credit, sharing the sinking with carrier aircraft.[4]

Table 3.4 War Patrol #4 Torpedo Summary						
Attack 1						
Tube	Track	Gyro	Depth	Hit/Miss	Erratic	Type
1	53° P	3° 30' L	5'	Hit	Normal	Mk. 23
2	53° P	3° 40' L	5'	Hit	Normal	Mk. 23
3	53° P	4° 10' L	5'	Hit	Normal	Mk. 23
Attack 2						
7	140° P	136°	3'	Miss	---	Mk. 18
8	141° P	137° 30'	3'	Miss	---	Mk. 18
9	142° P	144° 30'	3'	Miss	---	Mk. 18
10	068° S	150° 30'	3'	Miss	---	Mk. 18
Attack 3						
7	101° S	182°	3'	Hit	No	Mk. 18
8	104° S	183°	4'	Hit	No	Mk. 18

War Patrol #5

Batfish's fifth patrol was from October 8 to December 1, 1944 with a patrol area in the South China and Sulu Seas. The Navy designated this patrol as successful for the Combat Insignia Award where Fyfe fired twenty-one torpedoes, hitting with five of them. Fyfe sank four ships for 9,300 tons and damaged two other ships for 4,300 tons. However, the official JANAC total for this patrol was no ships sunk and no ships damaged.

Patrol No. 5
Torpedo Attack No. 1
Date: 19 October. Time: 2030
Lat. 6-45S, Long: 118-30E

As *Batfish* patrolled in the Flores Sea, radar made contact on one ship and two escorts. The target was a MFM design approximately three hundred feet in length and a minimum draft of approximately two feet. The foremast was sixty-two feet above the water line and the ship had a very high free board and a high stack with the bridge amidships. Tarpaulins covered guns and the ship had sound gear. At first, Fyfe thought the ship was a stripped cargo ship. Fast, light screws were making two hundred turns for nine knots, and the target was heading 095° at a range varying between 2,800 and 2,950 yards. At the time of the attack, *Batfish* was on the surface, making four knots on course 010°.

This attack was a night radar attack with the initial contact at 18,000 yards. Sea conditions were about a two. The target was steering a steady course of 095° at 9.5 knots. At 12,000 yards, two escort pips appeared on the radar and plot showed they were patrolling station on each side of target about 1,000 yards off its track. At 10,000 yards, sound heard echo ranging and at 5,000 yards sound picked up the ships screws. The target became visible from the bridge at 4,500 yards, appeared to be riding high, and was quite large. Due to this fact, and that the radar pip was so large at extreme ranges, Fyfe decided he had a tanker and therefore determined to let him have a full salvo. Fyfe had a perfect set up and fired six bow tubes, using a 1° spread, for a 2,600-yard torpedo run. The starboard tracks varied between 090° to 095°. Torpedo depths were set at four feet on tubes two, four and six and six feet on tubes one, three and five (Table 3.5). All torpedoes ran under the target. Fyfe later identified the ship as a "Q" ship, designed to lure submarines to attack, only to become the victim of a lethal counterattack.[5]

Patrol No. 5
Torpedo Attack No. 2
Date: 20 October. Time: 0036
Lat. 6-45S, Long: 119-00E

After missing the "tanker" on the previous attack, Fyfe maneuvered *Batfish* back into position to make another attack on this ship. The target was still making nine knots on a course of 095°. The range to the target was 2,855 yards. *Batfish*, on course 183° was making three knots on the surface.

The second attack on this target was a radar surface approach. Fyfe fired a very carefully aimed torpedo from tube number ten on a 90° starboard track. Fyfe set the torpedo to run at a depth of one foot. The torpedo broached about thirty to fifty yards from the ship; however, it then apparently ran hot, straight and normal (Table 3.5). The torpedo missed the primary target, but an explosion three minutes and forty seconds after firing may have sunk the far escort, an unidentified patrol craft of about three hundred tons. Although those on the bridge did not see the escort, two minutes later the port escort disappeared from the radar screen. This, and the fact that it stopped echo ranging at the time of the explosion, led Fyfe to believe he may have sunk the escort vessel. JANAC, however, did not give official credit for damaging or sinking this vessel.

Patrol No. 5
Torpedo Attack No. 3
Date: 6 November. Time: 1224
Lat. 16-27N, Long: 119-51E

Fyfe attacked a large cargo ship in a convoy of thirteen ships, one of which was an *Aoga*-class heavy cruiser with seven escorts. The convoy, proceeding up the west coast of Luzon, was heading for San Fernando Harbor. The cargo ship, with a draft of about twelve feet, was making 3.5 knots on a course varying between 010° and 015° and at a range between 2,290 and 2,320 yards. At the time of the attack, *Batfish* was at periscope depth, making three knots on a course ranging from 068° to 051°.

Fyfe conducted a periscope attack on the convoy with the original approach made on the heavy cruiser. A destroyer escort on the inner anti-submarine screen prevented the attack, forcing *Batfish* down to one hundred and twenty feet. After returning to periscope depth, Fyfe made a quick set up on a large cargo ship. Sound indicated that the target had slowed, so Fyfe fired six torpedoes from the bow tubes using a large spread to cover all possible speed errors. All torpedoes were set to a 120° port track; all were set for eight feet with an estimated run of 2,300 yards (Table 3.5). However, as Fyfe fired his torpedoes, the target changed course slowly to the right and continued the turn during the torpedo run. Even with the torpedo spread set to the target's length by periscope, all of them crossed ahead of the cargo ship. The development of a quick counterattack by escorting ships prevented Fyfe from firing the aft tubes.

Patrol No. 5
Torpedo Attack No. 4
Date: 12 November. Time: 1424
Lat. 16-38N, Long: 120-18E

On this attack, Fyfe damaged a 4,000-ton unidentified cargo ship. On November 12, Fyfe sighted one large, anchored cargo ship and two medium cargo ships moored to a dock in San Fernando Harbor. There were no anti-submarine crafts patrolling the entrance to the harbor and there were no anti-submarine nets or booms visible. In addition, there was no immediate activity on the nearby airfield.

Fyfe, with *Batfish* at periscope depth, traveling at three knots on course 160°, made an approach from the north in order to attack the ships in San Fernando Harbor. The large cargo ship at anchor and the two medium-sized cargo ships were all oriented about 330°. During the approach, *Batfish* experienced a strong easterly current that was cause of some concern. After running into the twenty-fathom curve, Fyfe decided to fire the torpedoes, because 1,000 yards closer in, the ocean bottom shoaled rapidly to fifty feet and he wanted to leave some room for an escape. Fyfe fired torpedoes at the anchored cargo ship from tubes three and four on a 20° starboard track and at a range of 2,500 yards. Fyfe aimed each torpedo by periscope, one at MOT and one just ahead of the bow to allow for the current. Fyfe fired two more torpedoes, one from tube one, set on low power and the other from tube two, towards the moored cargo ship on a 15° starboard track with a range of 4,800 yards (Table 3.5). Fyfe watched the first two torpedoes pass under stern of target and explode on the beach. Planes forced *Batfish* down before the third and fourth torpedoes reached the moored cargo ship, preventing visual confirmation. However, sound heard one solid hit five minutes and twenty-eight seconds after firing tube number one. Fyfe believed this torpedo hit either the moored cargo ship or the dock. JANAC did not give any official credit for this attack.

Patrol No. 5
Torpedo Attack No. 5
Date: 15 November. Time: 0025
Lat. 18N, Long: 118E

Fyfe attacked and sank an unidentified medium-sized 4,000-ton cargo ship. This torpedo attack five also sank an unidentified 1,000-ton destroyer escort. Patrolling as part of a coordinated attack group with *Ray* (SS 271) and *Raton* (SS 270), the three submarines intercepted a convoy of at least eight ships. *Raton* made the initial contact. *Batfish* tracked from ahead while the other two submarines attacked the convoy. *Ray* delivered the first attack from the convoy's port flank and sank a cargo ship carrying gasoline.

Shortly thereafter, *Raton* attacked from the convoy's starboard flank. At 2245, Fyfe received word from *Ray* that he was clear and for *Batfish* to attack from the convoy's port flank.

The remnants of the convoy consisted of four ships, represented by two small, one medium and one large pip on the radar screen. The convoy had reformed, was proceeding at 7.2 knots on a base course of 350° and was radically altering course from 335° to 045° on three-, four-, and six-minute legs. *Batfish* was on the surface, traveling at 3.7 knots on course 300°, trying to make a night radar attack with surface haze and no moon. The range to target was 6,500 yards astern and Fyfe began his approach on the largest pip. Fyfe finally sighted the target from the bridge at a range 4,700 yards. The ship appeared to be a medium-sized maru with quite a bit of superstructure and was smoking heavily, but was otherwise unidentifiable as to type, size, and age. Fyfe estimated it was a cargo ship or a combination cargo/transport ship. The escort appeared to be a large PC, a destroyer escort or a small destroyer.

Unexpected course changes by the target thwarted the first two attempts to get in firing position. Since *Batfish* had no bow torpedoes Fyfe did not get into attack position until 0024 at which time he fired four stern tubes on a 70° port track and a 3,200-yard torpedo run. The torpedoes were set for six feet and gyros practically zero (Table 3.5). The bridge crew saw and heard two hits on the target, timed as second and third torpedoes. Three minutes later the target sank. Moments later, the bridge crew felt and heard one explosion, timed as the fourth torpedo to the far escort. At the same time, the escort's screws and echo ranging stopped and one minute later disappeared from the radar screen. This target was never in sight from the bridge. JANAC did not credit *Batfish* with either sinking.

Table 3.5 War Patrol #5 Torpedo Summary						
Attack 1						
Tube	Track	Gyro	Depth	Hit/Miss	Erratic	Type
1	91° S	356° 20'	6'	Miss	No	Mk. 23
2	92° S	356° 15'	6'	Miss	No	Mk. 23
3	93° S	359° 30'	6'	Miss	No	Mk. 23
4	95° S	356° 30'	6'	Miss	No	Mk. 23
5	95° S	002°	6'	Miss	No	Mk. 23

6	96° S	000° 30'	6'	Miss	No	Mk. 23
Attack 2						
10	92° S	180° 10'	1'	Hit	Broach	Mk. 18-1
Attack 3						
1	120° P	002°	8'	Miss	No	Mk. 23
2	122° P	004° 20'	8'	Miss	No	Mk. 23
3	120° P	009°	8'	Miss	No	Mk. 23
4	132° P	002° 30'	8'	Miss	No	Mk. 23
5	132° P	006°	8'	Miss	No	Mk. 23
6	132° P	009° 10'	8'	Miss	No	Mk. 23
Attack 4						
3	22° S	000° 25'	6'	Miss	No	Mk. 23
4	22° S	000° 35'	6'	Miss	No	Mk. 23
1	15° S	352° 10'	6'	Hit	No	14-3A
2	16° S	352° 40'	6'	Miss	No	Mk. 23
Attack 5						
7	69° P	176°	6'	Miss	No	Mk. 18-1
8	70° P	175° 30'	6'	Hit	No	Mk. 18-1
9	70° P	175°	6'	Hit	No	Mk. 18-1
10	69° P	171°	6'	Hit[a]	No	Mk. 18-1

a: Timed as hit on far escort and not primary target

War Patrol #6

Batfish's sixth patrol was from December 30, 1944 to March 3, 1945 with its patrol area in the South China Sea and Luzon Straits. The Navy designated this patrol as successful for the Combat Insignia Award where Fyfe fired seventeen torpedoes, hitting with five of them. Fyfe sank three ships for 4,500 tons and damaged one ship for 200 tons. The official total for this patrol was three ships sunk for 3,262 tons and no ships damaged.

Patrol No. 6
Gun Attack No. 1
Date: 23 January. Time: 0711(H)
Lat. 20-10N, Long: 111-44E

SJ radar made initial contact with two pips at 9,800 yards. Targets tracked on course 180° with speeds varying between one and three knots. Fyfe eased in to 3,500 yards and spotted two large shapes from the bridge, but sound could not hear screws or echo ranging. Since the pips were rather small, Fyfe decided they could be one of a dozen things and not wishing to give the submarine away to the expected convoy, he decided to track them until daylight and make a submerged approach if they were actual targets.

After observing approximately twenty-eight targets from periscope depth during daylight, Fyfe identified them as Chinese Junks so he surfaced with intentions of stopping the group and searching for contraband. Firing started at 3,000 yards and ceased at 2,000 yards. After firing a few rounds, all vessels stopped and hove to. The submarine went alongside four Junks taken at random and found them to be harmless Chinese fishermen. Fyfe noted damage on one of the ships, so he gave the crew of the Junk provisions as evidence of their good intentions and sent a boarding party and pharmacist mate aboard the one they had hit to give any aid possible. The damage by *Batfish* to the Junk was three holes in hull, the aft mast shot down, and some of the rigging partially demolished.

Patrol No. 6
Gun Attack No. 2
Date: 4 February. Time: 1745(H)
Lat. 21-00N, Long: 119-50E

While proceeding on the surface in heavy weather and low visibility, lookouts spotted a small vessel on a northwesterly course at about 4,500 yards. After closing, Fyfe identified the ship as a Japanese Landing Barge estimated at about 175 tons. Because of the heavy weather, the crew was not able to use the five-inch deck gun, so Fyfe closed to 1,200 yards and opened fire with the 40mm gun. The target returned fire with a light machine gun so Fyfe closed to about 500 yards and made several strafing runs with the 20mm and .50 caliber machine guns. On one occasion, the target attempted to ram the submarine but at other times attempted to keep it on his stern.

The 40mm gun hit the target about forty or fifty times, catching on fire twice, but the flames did not take hold, probably due to heavy seas and the light rain. Fyfe closed to within fifty to seventy-five yards and strafed the target from point blank range and in spite of poor visibility, Fyfe observed numerous large holes. Since it had turned dark and the target was not visible at fifty yards, Fyfe decided to break off the attack, believing *Batfish's* guns killed or mortally wounded all personnel. Fyfe doubted that the vessel could ever make port with sea conditions being what they were, with the vessel's condition being what it was, and the nearest land eighty miles to the north. JANAC did not award credit for damaging this vessel as it was below the 500-ton limit.

Patrol No. 6
Torpedo Attack No. 1
Date: 31 January. Time: 1026(H)
Lat. 16-07N, Long: 109-37E

Fyfe attacked a small MFM cargo ship proceeding close in to the beach along the south coast of Hainan between Gaalong Bay and Yulinkan Bay. A medium sized tug and a smaller vessel, probably a pilot boat, were standing off the entrance to Yulin. The target had a draft of four feet, was traveling at nine knots on course 250° and was at a range of 1,110 yards. *Batfish* was at periscope depth, proceeding on course 350° at 2.5 knots.

Fyfe made a normal periscope approach against the small cargo ship. The target was against the land background and did not spot the ship until the range was 8,000 yards. Prior to firing, sonar set a single ping to confirm the range to target, which agreed with the range generated by the TDC. With a perfect set up and all data generating beautifully, Fyfe fired three Mark 18-2 torpedoes from the bow tubes on an 98° port track, using a 3° divergent spread (Table 3.6). The range to target was 1,000 yards and all torpedoes were set to run at four feet. At the start of the approach, Fyfe ordered a two foot depth setting. Fyfe apparently misidentified the target as he unfortunately assumed the target's draft was greater and with the state three seas unsuitable for firing torpedoes with shallower settings, Fyfe increased the depth setting to four feet. Sound tracked all torpedoes to, under and away from target.

Patrol No. 6
Torpedo Attack No. 2
Date: 9 February. Time: 2330(H)
Lat. 18-50N, Long: 121-33E

Fyfe attacked a surfaced Japanese submarine, later identified as a Japanese I-class submarine. SJ radar made contact at an initial range of 11,000 yards. The target was proceeding on course 310° at a speed of twelve knots toward the pass between Fuga and Caniguin Islands on a direct course from Cape Batulinao. *Batfish* was on the surface, moving at five knots on course 269°.

The night was dark and overcast with no moon so Fyfe decided to attack on the surface, using radar, if possible. Since the horizon was darkest to the east, Fyfe attacked from that direction. At 2330, Fyfe fired four Mark 18-2 torpedoes from the bow tubes using 2° divergent spread. The range to the target was 1,850 yards and the torpedoes were set to run at six feet with an average track angle 145° starboard (Table 3.6). All torpedoes missed astern and sound heard them explode at the end of run eight minutes later. It was later determined the target was traveling at fourteen knots and not twelve. The target never showed any indications of being aware of *Batfish* neither did it become alerted by the end of run explosions. It may have assumed these were bombing attacks on northern Luzon. Fyfe pulled off the track of the Japanese submarine and started a new approach.

Patrol No. 6
Torpedo Attack No. 3
Date: 10 February. Time: 0002(H)
Lat. 18-56N, Long: 121-34E

Fyfe attacked the same Japanese submarine attacked previously in Attack #2. After opening out from the target's track following the first attack on this target, Fyfe started another end around. The target tracked at fourteen knots and shortly after Fyfe started the approach, the target changed base course to 020° in order to clear Fuga Island. At the time of the attack, the target had a draft of sixteen feet and was at a range of 990 yards. *Batfish* was traveling at five knots on course 290° and Fyfe was going to attack on the surface using radar. Another deciding factor to stay on the surface was that the target's radar was either not very efficient or else it was anti-aircraft only. Again, Fyfe utilized the favorable dark background to the east.

The Japanese submarine was now visible from bridge as the range to the target decreased to 1,500 yards. When the range closed to 1,020 yards, Fyfe identified the target as an I-class Japanese submarine. At the beginning of the approach, Fyfe ordered the torpedoes set at depths of four feet, two feet and two feet on a 90° starboard track. As the gyros started to increase, Fyfe commenced firing. The first torpedo was a hot run in the tube, it did not eject but it did start running. On a second try it did eject, but probably ran erratic. The second torpedo, fired on a 115° starboard track with a 30° right gyro and a range to target of 920 yards, hit the target. The Japanese submarine exploded with a brilliant red flame and sank almost immediately leaving a large oil slick that extended over a radius of two miles. The third torpedo tracked to the target, but there was nothing left for it to hit and exploded at the end of its run eight minutes later (Table 3.6). Sound heard secondary explosions three minutes after the attack, believed to be internal explosions from the target. The Japanese submarine was a 1,500-ton I-Class submarine that JANAC officially credited as the 2,212-ton *I-41*. There is controversy surrounding the identity of this Japanese submarine, which is the topic of Chapter 5: Mistaken Identity.

Patrol No. 6
Torpedo Attack No. 4
Date: 11 February. Time: 2202(H)
Lat. 18-53N, Long: 121-47E

Fyfe attacked and sank another 1,500-ton Japanese submarine. SJ radar made initial contact at a range of 8,000 yards with a Japanese submarine heading on a southeasterly course towards the vicinity of Batulinao Bay. The target tracked on base course 135°, with a constant helming of 15° right and left and at a speed of seven knots. At the time of attack, the target was on course 120° traveling at twelve knots and the range to the target was 880 yards. *Batfish* was at radar depth, making three knots on course 021°.

In view of the previous night's success against a similar target, Fyfe decided to attack on surface. Fyfe had favorable lighting conditions with no moon, a partially overcast sky and rain squalls behind the submarine. At a range of 1,800 yards, Fyfe sighted the target from the bridge, and by the time the range had decreased to 1,200 yards, he identified is as a Japanese submarine. Fyfe could not ascertain the exact class of the target, but he believed it to be similar to the I-class submarine in the previous attack. About one minute before Fyfe was to commence firing, the target dove, only to surface twenty minutes later. SJ radar regained contact at 8,650 yards, so Fyfe started a new approach and worked up ahead of the target, diving to radar depth.

The target now tracked on base course 120° at a speed of twelve knots. At a range of 880 yards, Fyfe fired four Mark 18-2 torpedoes from the bow tubes, set to run at four feet, and on a 70° starboard track, 15° left gyros, using a one-knot speed spread (Table 3.6). The first torpedo hit after a timed run to target of fifty seconds and the target sank almost immediately. The second and third torpedoes also hit but with a muffled explosion that indicated they had detonated by hitting a piece of the target or by the disturbance caused by the initial hit. Five minutes after firing, sound heard two loud explosions from the direction of the target and one more explosion four minutes later. Fyfe interpreted these as internal explosions marking the end of this particular ship. The fourth torpedo exploded at the end of an eight-minute run. JANAC officially credited this submarine as the 525-ton *RO-112*.

Tube	Track	Gyro	Depth	Hit/Miss	Erratic	Type
Table 3.6 War Patrol #6 Torpedo Summary						
Attack 1						
1	96° P	350° 30'	4'	Miss	No	Mk. 18-2
2	98° P	351° 50'	4'	Miss	No	Mk. 18-2
3	104° P	50° 20'	4'	Miss	No	Mk. 18-2
Attack 2						
1	145° S	010.5°	6'	Miss	No	Mk. 18-2
2	145° S	010°	6'	Miss	No	Mk. 18-2
3	145° S	009° 40'	6'	Miss	No	Mk. 18-2
4	150° S	011° 10'	6'	Miss	No	Mk. 18-2
Attack 3						
1	107° S	019° 10'	4'	Miss	Yes	Mk. 18-2
2	115° S	033° 10'	2'	Hit	No	Mk. 18-2
3	125° S	038° 30'	2'	Miss	No	Mk. 18-2

			Attack 4			
1	62° S	341°	4'	Hit	No	Mk. 18-2
2	64° S	341° 10'	4'	Hit	No	Mk. 18-2
3	68° S	346° 30'	4'	Hit	No	Mk. 18-2
4	76° S	354° 10'	4'	Miss	No	Mk. 18-2
			Attack 5			
7	76° S	175° 30'	6'	Hit	No	Mk. 18-2
9	75° S	174° 30'	6'	Miss	No	Mk. 18-2
10	80° S	179° 30'	6'	Miss	No	Mk. 18-2

Patrol No. 6
Torpedo Attack No. 5
Date: 13 February. Time: 0448(H)
Lat. 19-10N, Long: 121-25E

Fyfe attacked and sank another 1,500-ton Japanese submarine. Radar made initial contact at a range of 10,700 yards and Fyfe started his approach on the target that was proceeding at six knots on a southeasterly course between Calayan and Dalupiri Islands. Twenty-six minutes later, with the range to the target at 7,150 yards, the Japanese submarine dove. The target had tracked on base course 120°, so Fyfe headed for a spot ahead of and on its track to be in position for an attack before dawn in the event that the Japanese submarine surfaced again. One hour and ten minutes after the target dove, the submarine surfaced and SJ radar regained contact at a range of 9,600 yards. Fyfe started a new approach.

With the range to target down to 6,800 yards, Fyfe submerged *Batfish* on the target's track and continued the approach from radar depth. With only two torpedoes in the forward torpedo room, Fyfe swung *Batfish* around for an aft shot. At the time of the attack, the Japanese submarine had a draft of sixteen feet, was making six knots on course 140° and was at a range of 1,700 yards. *Batfish* was at radar depth, making three knots on course 220°. As the range decreased, Fyfe fired three Mark 18-2 torpedoes from the aft tubes on an 80° starboard track, zero gyros and a torpedo run of 1,500 yards. The torpedoes were set to run at six feet and with a one-knot speed spread (Table 3.6). All torpedoes ran hot, straight, and normal. Fyfe saw one torpedo hit the submarine, which blew the target apart causing it to sink in less than ten seconds. A brilliant orange explosion accompanied the hit. A wide diffusion of pips on the radar screen indicated the submarine literally blew apart. The other two torpedoes tracked to the target but with nothing there to hit, they both exploded at the end of their runs. Fyfe searched the wreckage and recovered several books, papers, and equipment. A heavy oil slick spread over a large area and nearly two hours after the attack, oil was still bubbling to surface in the spot where the target sank. JANAC officially credited this target as the 525-ton *RO-113*.

War Patrol #7

Batfish's seventh and last patrol was from June 26, 1945 to August 22, 1945 with its patrol area around the Southeast Coast of Kyushu. LCDR Walter L. Small relieved Fyfe of command on March 17, 1945. The Navy designated this patrol as successful for the Combat Insignia Award where Small did not fire any torpedoes. The highlights of this patrol were one town shelled with moderate damage and the rescue of three downed aviators, discussed in Chapter 6: Salvation.

Patrol No. 7
Gun Attack No. 1
Date: 24 July. Time: 1926
Lat. 30-25N, Long: 130-23E

By this time in the war, targets were hard to come by and many patrols centered around lifeguard duty for carrier and land-based bombing raids on the Japanese mainland. Therefore, Small did not have the opportunity to perform a torpedo attack during this patrol. However, he was able to initiate one gun attack against a small coastal town of Nagata on Yaku Shima.

Gun crews fired twenty-five rounds 5"/25 and one hundred and twenty-eight rounds 40mm. The 40mm opened fire at a range of 3,500 yards, and put practically all of its shells in the target area. The five-inch gun opened fire on the barracks and camp area at the right end of the beach. Gun crews observed one direct hit on barbed wire entanglements and one hit that demolished a frame building in the camp area. After ten rounds, thick smoke and dust prevented further fall of shot, therefore the five-inch gun shifted to the town. The gun crew reported one direct hit on a building and after about nine rounds smoke and dust again prevented spotting, so the five-inch gun shifted back to the camp area which had cleared a little. These last shots all fell directly in the camp with one hit on a building and one round bursting directly on the barracks. The average five-inch gun range was around 5,000 yards. About 90% of the shells fell within the target area and there were probably several other hits which could not be observed because of the smoke. The final count was one building destroyed, two and possibly more buildings and barbed wire entanglements damaged. Smoke and haze prevented further observation of fall of shot.

Conclusion

Batfish made seven war patrols with three different commanders (Table 3.7). Merrill commanded during patrols one and two and sank two ships but with only one officially credited. The reduction in numbers is due, in part to a poor second patrol, hampered by bad weather and lack of shipping. Fyfe was the skipper for the third, fourth, fifth and sixth patrols and was the submarines' most successful captain; sinking fourteen ships with JANAC only crediting him with six. He was probably the most aggressive of the three with his tactics and results supporting this observation. He commanded *Batfish's* famous sixth patrol sinking a record three Japanese submarines in approximately seventy-six hours. Small was the last of the World War II captains, commanding *Batfish* on patrol seven, sinking no ships, but rescuing three downed aviators. Small appeared to be an aggressive skipper, but timing did not favor him as by the time he was in command, a lack of Japanese shipping and the end of the war prevented him from conducting torpedo attacks in *Batfish*.

Table 3.7 Captain Comparisons							
Captain	War Patrols	Torpedoes		Sunk (Claimed)	Sunk (Official)	Ships Damaged	Aviators Rescued
		Fired	Hits				
Merrill	1, 2	8	5	2	1	0	0
Fyfe	3, 4, 5, 6	63	19	14	6	3	0
Small	7	0	0	0	0	0	3

As seen in the preceding narrative and as visualized in Table 3.8, what *Batfish* skippers attacked and reported sunk was not necessarily correct. This was an issue with all submarines operating in the Pacific in World

War II. What submarines reported as sinking did not mean it sank; and if it actually did sink, JANAC did not necessarily credit it as sinking. This discrepancy is best explanation this way:

> A major problem exists in evaluating submarine attacks because of the very nature of submarine warfare. Submarine commanding officers are not usually able to make positive identification of their targets or to verify the extent of damage caused by an attack. War records are replete with examples of submarine commanders who believed they had witnessed sinkings only to find out later that they had been deceived by premature explosions of their torpedoes. It was even more common for commanders to overestimate the size of their targets, in part because of the magnification provided by periscope lenses and also because of the limited opportunity to examine a target ship. Submarine officers also tended to over estimate damage based on unseen explosions or "breaking-up" noises heard by sonar.[6]

This is very evident with *Batfish* when looking at what the skippers thought they attacked and sank versus what JANAC actually credited. In actuality, *Batfish's* sinking total should be somewhat higher due to the vivid description and eyewitness testimony of the patrol reports. Nevertheless, the official JANAC total stands and *Batfish* sits in the middle of the pack with seven ships sunk.

Table 3.8 War Patrol Results - Detail			
Patrol	**Date**	**Claimed (Ship/Tonnage)**	**Official (Ship/Tonnage)**
1	1/2044	Ginyo Maru (8,613)	Hidaka Maru (5,486)
	1/20/44	Tatukami Maru (7,065)	- - -
2	- - -	- - -	- - -

3	6/10/44	Unknown ship (3,500)	- - -
	6/18/44	Mayati Maru (2,232)	- - -
	6/22/44	Anastasia Maru (3,110)	Nagaragawa Maru (990)
	7/1/44	Isuzugawa Maru #5 (226)	- - -
	7/1/44	Kamoi or Kamo Maru (138)	- - -
4	8/23/44	Minekaze Class DD (1200)	Minesweeper W22 (492)
	8/26/44	Fubuki Class DD (1500)	Samidare (1,580)
5	10/20/44	Unidentified PC (300)	- - -
	11/12/44	Unidentified AK (4,000)	- - -
	11/15/44	Unidentified AK (4,000)	- - -
	11/15/44	Unidentified DE (1,000)	- - -
6	2/10/45	I Class Submarine (1,500)	I-41 (2,212)
	2/11/45	I Class Submarine (1,500)	RO-112 (525)
	2/13/45	I Class Submarine (1,500)	RO-113 (525)
7	- - -	- - -	- - -

Chapter 4: The Hunter Hunted

The purpose of an anti-submarine weapon in World War II was to sink an enemy submarine by rupturing the pressure hull.[1] In most cases, surface ships such as destroyers or destroyer escorts would locate and attack a submerged submarine with depth charges producing a pressure shock wave with enough force to rupture the pressure hull. However, if a submarine launched a torpedo at another submarine, the torpedo warhead carried enough explosive charge to not only rupture the hull, but also would usually destroy and sink the target submarine.[2]

A submarine on the surface or to a lesser extent at periscope depth was vulnerable to torpedoes fired by other submarines. When aircraft attacked a surfaced submarine, the submarine could often dive quickly enough to avoid the attack if a sharp visual or electronic lookout was being kept. Not so if a submerged submarine attacked a surfaced submarine; there would be no warning.[3] In the 1920's, General William "Billy" Mitchell said, "The best defense against submarines is other submarines."[4] Ironically, the first enemy warship sunk by a U.S. submarine was the Japanese submarine *I-73*, a victim of *Gudgeon* (SS 211) on January 27, 1942.[5]

A combination of stealth, skill, aggressiveness and technology played an integral part in helping an American submarine contact, approach and attack an enemy submarine. Even so, one must consider if luck played a minor role. Consider the vastness of the Pacific Ocean and the relatively small size of a submarine:

> Given the immensity of the world's oceans and the relative smallness of a submarine, it is surprising how often submarines found each other. One boat would spot

the other, make a short approach, fire torpedoes and hope they ran true. With a decisiveness rarely seen in warfare, in these engagements there was almost always a winner and a loser. The winner lived to fight another day; the loser most often sank. The engagements were generally brief and violent.[6]

Throughout World War II, U.S fleet submarines were very capable anti-submarine weapons. Fyfe in *Batfish* demonstrated this by showing that a submarine, with the right set of conditions, could effectively attack and sink an enemy submarine.

How effective was a U.S. fleet submarine in World War II when it came to anti-submarine warfare? Submarines were neither specifically employed for anti-submarine duty nor were Japanese submarines very high on the target priority list from 1942 to 1945. There were exceptions, for example, when *Corvina* (SS 226), *Drum* (SS 228) and *Blackfish* received an ULTRA message of a passing Japanese submarine near Truk.[7] Joe's Jugheads serve as another example when *Batfish* and the other wolf pack submarines were seeking Japanese submarines transporting personnel from Luzon to Formosa.

Fyfe ultimately sank three Japanese submarines in approximately seventy-six hours. This was the most by any one United States fleet submarine during World War II. Many submarines had one, a few had two, but only *Batfish* had three. In fact, as mentioned earlier, only one other Allied submarine, H.M.S. *Upholder*, made the same claim of sinking three enemy submarines.[8] What tactics did Fyfe in *Batfish* use to sink these enemy submarines in what has to be one of the best examples of a submarine conducting anti-submarine warfare?

A key component when attacking a surfaced submarine is that the situation could get complicated quickly, as the target submarine was not limited to two dimensions. In other words, it could submerge, at which point it could drastically alter course, speed and depth in an attempt to escape and avoid or, more worrisome to the attacking submarine, to launch a counter attack.[9]

Submarine vs. submarine! The hunter hunted! The biggest fear of a submarine sailor during World War II was that an enemy submarine might get the drop on them while they were making a passage on the surface.[10]

In the Pacific Theater, surface ships and aircraft were responsible for sinking seventy-three and twenty-two submarines, respectively. Overall, the Japanese lost 131 submarines to all causes.[11] The number of Japanese submarines lost due to attacks by Allied submarines varies. Some claims indicate that sixteen Japanese submarines were lost from submarine attacks.[12] Others say the number was twenty.[13] Still others push the number to twenty-five (twenty-three Japanese and two German).[14] This equates to almost twenty percent of Japanese submarines sunk by American submarines. In contrast, the only American submarine positively known sunk by a Japanese submarine was *Corvina* on November 26, 1943. Ironically, *Corvina* was lost due to an attack by *I-176*, the Japanese submarine *Corvina* was sent to sink.[15]

The true number of Japanese submarines sunk by U.S. submarines may actually be much higher. Documented attacks by American submarines on Japanese submarines clearly describe the sinking of the target. For example, *Archerfish* (SS 311) on February 14, 1945 attacked and sank a surfaced Japanese submarine.[16] Yet post-war records do not credit *Archerfish* with the sinking and they do not show the loss of a Japanese submarine at the time of that attack. This record keeping example may be the norm instead of the exception and will probably be an issue that never gets resolved.

For more than a decade after World War I, American submarine policy, design and construction was based on the attitude that the submarine had value only in coastal defense and for support operations of the battle fleet. These support operations were to report enemy movements and carry out torpedo attacks on the enemy battle fleet.[17] Clearly, early American naval strategists failed to heed the lessons from World War I in developing a commerce-destroying submarine.

In May 1941, the Naval War College conducted a study involving submarines as commerce raiders, a role they were well suited for, and urged the Navy to use submarines in that fashion; however, the Navy rejected the study. Even though pre-war strategic naval doctrine did not include the idea of warfare on commerce, it only took a slight shift of viewpoint to use the submarine in this way: Pearl Harbor.[18]

At one stroke, the battleship fleet, upon which naval planners counted on to carry the main weight in a war against Japan, lay in ruins. As the Japanese expanded into the southwest Pacific, submarines struck at lines of communication and supply as well as Japanese capital shipping.[19] After the Battle of Midway, the Japanese juggernaut stalled and American submarines seized the offensive. Released from defensive duties, the thrust of the submarine campaign was the vital sea lanes around Japan, ultimately taking a heavy toll on Japanese shipping.[20]

With this shift in philosophy, submarines took on more of an aggressive role rather than that of fleet support. The navy developed new tactics with the goal to sink enemy commerce shipping such as supply and troop ships, tankers, and of course capital ships if possible. The best position for the submarine to be when attacking a ship was directly ahead of the target so that it could maneuver into a favorable firing position. When making that attack, the submarine could utilize a variety of different methods, all of which were dependent on the time of day, weather, and lighting conditions.

A day periscope attack involved a submerged submarine using its periscope to visually identify, track and attack the target.[21] During a night periscope attack the submarine would usually track the target on the surface and submerge to periscope depth ahead and on the track of the approaching ship.[22]

Once the navy installed surface search radar on submarines, it became possible to identify targets outside of visual range. On the darkest nights or during adverse weather conditions, it was now possible to obtain accurate ranges, speed and an estimate of the number of ships.[23] A radar-visual night attack was generally conducted on the surface allowing the submarine to use radar to approach the enemy until the bridge crew made visual contact. For this type of attack to be successful, the night must be dark. Bright moonlight would necessitate a night periscope attack to prevent the enemy from spotting the submarine.[24]

A submerged submarine could use a combination of radar and the periscope. Many factors decided whether to use this method; however, the deciding factor was on visibility. A submarine could submerge to radar depth, generally around forty-two feet, and still use the periscope to identify and track the enemy.[25] This type of attack was not very popular among skippers.[26] Battle experience proved a great many pre-war ideas about night visibility wrong. For example, the idea that the sector toward the moon is always the sector of best visibility was often not the case. Usually, the sector of best visibility was where the greatest contrast between color of sky and water existed, producing a well-defined horizon. More often than not, the sectors bordering the path of the moon were the sectors of poorest visibility.[27]

A submarine would stay on the surface during the night surface attack, using a combination of radar and visual observations.[28] Throughout the war, this method was the most productive type of attack.[29] Usually employed during a night radar approach, submarines employed the minimum silhouette method that kept the bow of the submarine pointed at the target, reducing the probability of being sighted.[30] As illustrated in *Batfish's* sixth war patrol report (Appendices 1, 2 and 3), Fyfe in *Batfish* used a combination of these methods in addition to skill, aggressiveness, technology and even some luck as he attacked three Japanese submarines.[31]

Fyfe attacked the first Japanese submarine on February 9-10, 1945 (Figure 4.1). Both submarines were on the surface and the target was proceeding northward toward the pass between Fuga and Camiguin Islands at a speed of twelve knots on a direct course from northern Luzon. First indications of a target was a steady 158 megacycles (mgcs), 500 pulse repetition frequency (PRF) radar signal that rapidly became louder and reached saturation shortly after contact was made. This was indicative of Japanese air-search radar. *Batfish's* surface search radar initially contacted the Japanese submarine at 11,000 yards, tracked on course 310° and at a speed of twelve knots. *Batfish* was traveling at five knots on course 269°.

The night was dark with no moon and a partially overcast sky, so Fyfe decided to make a night radar attack on surface if possible. The horizon was darkest to the east so Fyfe attacked from that direction. At 2330, Fyfe fired four Mark 18-2 torpedoes from the bow tubes at a range of 1,850 yards. Torpedoes were set to run at a depth of six feet with an average track angle 145° starboard and gyros angles of 10° right using 2° divergent spread. Due to a two-knot speed error, all torpedoes missed astern and sound heard them explode at their end of run eight minutes later. Surprisingly the target at no time showed any indications that it was aware of the *Batfish's* presence.

Fyfe pulled off the targets track and started a new approach. Shortly thereafter, the target, with its speed now resolved at fourteen knots, changed base course to 020° in order to clear Fuga Island. Fyfe decided to stay on the surface since, and judging from the first attack on this target, he concluded the Japanese submarines' radar was either not very efficient or else it was anti-aircraft only. *Batfish* was on course 290° traveling at five knots, and again utilized the favorable dark background to the east.

With range to target at 1,500 yards, the Japanese submarine was visible from bridge and when the ranged closed to 1,020 yards, Fyfe identified the target as an I-class Japanese submarine. The target was on the firing bearing for a 90° starboard track, and gyros had already started to increase so Fyfe commenced firing immediately. The first torpedo was a hot run

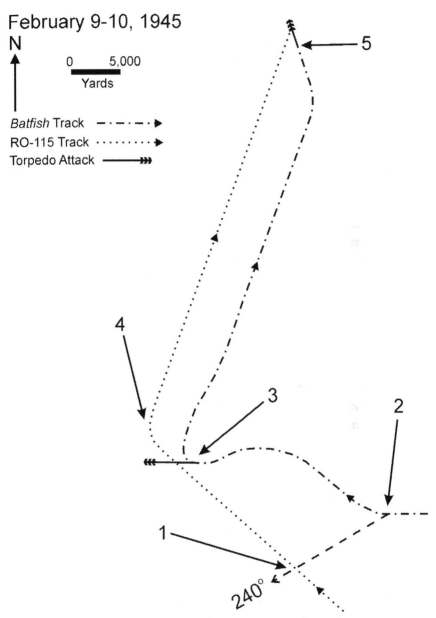

Figure 4.1. February 9-10 attack diagram. 1) SJ radar picks up Japanese submarine at 11,000 yards. 2) *Batfish* on course 269° when contact is made. 3) Fyfe fires four torpedoes, all miss. 4) Japanese submarine changes course to 020°. Fyfe begins end around. 5) Fyfe fires three torpedoes, sinks Japanese submarine.

in the tube. It fired on a second attempt but was already running and it probably ran erratic. The second torpedo, which Fyfe fired at a range of 920 yards on a 115° starboard track with a 30° right gyro, hit the target, which sank almost immediately. The third torpedo missed and exploded at the end of its run eight minutes later. Three minutes after the first torpedo hit the Japanese submarine, sound picked up secondary explosions, believed to be internal to the target.

Fyfe attacked a second submarine on February 11, 1945 (Figure 4.2). Both submarines were again on the surface and the target was on a southeasterly course heading for the vicinity of Batulinao Bay. The crew suspected the presence of a target when they picked up a radar signal on the APR at 158 mgcs that was rapidly getting louder. The target tracked on base course 135°. SJ radar made contact at 8,000 yards, thirty-six minutes after receiving the initial radar signal on APR. Plot confirmed the target was on course 135°, constant helming 15° right and left and at a speed of seven knots. In view of the previous success in a night surface attack against a similar target with similar radar, Fyfe decided to make attack on the surface in order to more fully identify the target as it was believed to be a Japanese submarine. There was no moon in the partially overcast sky and rain squalls behind *Batfish* provided favorable lighting conditions.

At a range of 1,800 yards, lookouts sighted the target from the bridge and as the range decreased to 1,200 yards, Fyfe identified the target as a Japanese submarine, similar to the I-class submarine sank the night before. About one minute before Fyfe commenced firing, the Japanese submarine submerged. The reason for this maneuver was unknown but by the process of elimination, Fyfe believed the crew of the Japanese submarine had either sighted or made radar contact on *Batfish*. Fyfe later thought that the submarine was only making a routine night dive. The latter was probably true as the Japanese submarine surfaced twenty minutes later. The first indication that he had surfaced was a noise, similar to that of a submarine blowing ballast tanks, coming from the direction of the target. Next, *Batfish* detected the Japanese submarines' 158 mgcs radar and finally SJ radar made contact at 8,650 yards. Fyfe started a new approach and worked up ahead of the target. With range to target at 6,000 yards, Fyfe submerged to radar depth. The target had increased speed from seven to twelve knots, and now tracked on base course 120°. *Batfish* was on course 021° traveling at three knots.

With a range of 880 yards, Fyfe commenced firing four Mark 18-2 torpedoes from the forward tubes on a 70° to 100° starboard track, 15° left

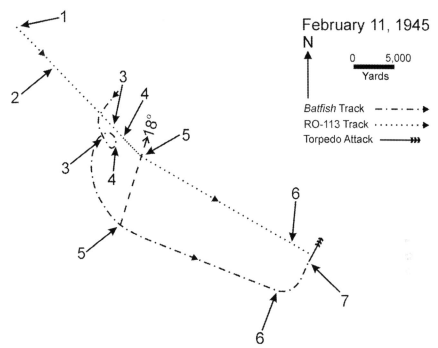

Figure 4.2. February 11 attack diagram. 1) Japanese submarine contact with APR on course 135°, 2) SJ radar contact established, 3) Japanese submarine sighted, 4) Japanese submarine submerged, 5) Target surfaces, contact re-established, 6) *Batfish* goes to radar depth, 7) Fyfe fires four torpedoes, sinking Japanese submarine.

gyros, using a one-knot speed spread. All torpedoes were set to run at four feet. The first torpedo hit after a timed run to target of fifty seconds and the submarine sank almost immediately. The second and third torpedoes also hit but with a muffled explosion that indicated they had detonated by hitting a piece of the target or by the disturbance caused by the initial hit. Five minutes after firing, two loud explosions from direction of the target and one more nine minutes after firing, interpreted as internal explosions marking the end of this particular ship. The fourth torpedo exploded at the end of an eight-minute run.

Fyfe attacked the third submarine on February 13, 1945 (Figure 4.3). The first indication of a target was again a weak APR signal on 157 mgcs, 500 PRF. From previous experience, Fyfe believed this to be another Japanese I-class submarine. The target was traveling at approximately seven knots on a southeasterly course between Calayan and Dalupiri Islands. The patrol report does not indicate weather conditions during this attack. By comparing the February 13 deck log against the February 10 and February 11 deck logs, it was determined that weather conditions were almost identical on all three nights with low cumulonimbus clouds covering up to eight-tenths of the sky with a ceiling of 16,000 feet.[32]

Twenty-six minutes later with range to target 7,150 yards on *Batfish's* starboard side, the target dove - reason unknown. The Japanese submarine had tracked on base course of 120° so Fyfe headed for a spot ahead of and on its track to be in position for an attack before dawn in the event that it surfaced again. Approximately thirty minutes after diving, the Japanese submarine surfaced as *Batfish* detected the APR signal at 157 mcgs. One hour and ten minutes after the submarine disappeared, and after a few bad moments when Fyfe thought the Japanese submarine was making an approach on them, *Batfish* regained contact. The target was at position 336° and at a range of 9,600 yards so Fyfe started a new approach. When the range to the submarine reached 6,800 yards, Fyfe submerged *Batfish* on the Japanese submarine's track and continued the approach from radar depth.

At this point in the patrol, there were only had two torpedoes in the forward torpedo room. Therefore, Fyfe swung *Batfish* around to bring the aft torpedo tubes to bear on the approaching Japanese submarine. At the time of firing, the Japanese submarine was on course 140° at six knots while *Batfish* headed on course 220° at three knots. Fyfe fired three Mark 18-2 torpedoes on an 80° starboard track with zero gyros angles, used a one-knot speed spread and all torpedo depths were set at six feet.. The torpedo run was 1,500 yards and all torpedoes ran hot, straight, and normal. A brilliant orange explosion accompanied the first torpedo hit followed by a wide diffusion of pips on the radar screen. The Japanese submarine literally blew apart. There was nothing left for the other two torpedoes to hit; they both exploded at the end of their run, more than nine minutes later.

Fyfe brought *Batfish* to the surface and headed for the oil slick and wreckage debris that remained after the sinking. The crew rigged up a searchlight to search the area but this was unproductive so Fyfe stayed on the surface until it was light enough to inspect the area. After sighting several bits of wood and paper, and a lot of oil, but no survivors, the search for something tangible was rewarded when a wooden box was recovered that contained Japanese navigation equipment and a book of tables. From the positions listed in the book, the Japanese submarine sailed from Nagoya to Formosa before heading south to Luzon.

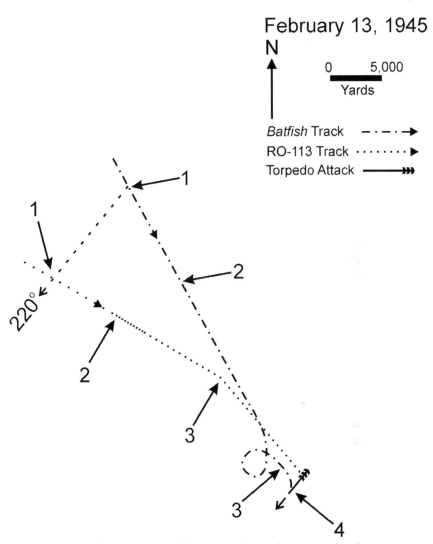

February 13, 1945

Figure 4.3. February 13 attack diagram. 1) SJ radar contact made at 10,700 yards, 2) Japanese submarine submerged, 3) Japanese submarine surface, contact regained, 4) *Batfish* submerges along target track, fires three torpedoes and sinks Japanese submarine.

How effective was a U.S. fleet submarine in World War II when it came to anti-submarine warfare? If the account from *Batfish's* sixth patrol is any example, they had the potential to be very effective weapons in anti-submarine operations. Fyfe made four attacks on three Japanese submarines, three of which were successful in sinking the targets. On each occasion, Fyfe used weather conditions and lighting to assist in keeping the submarine virtually invisible while on the surface. For example, Fyfe made night surface attacks on two of the three attacks as a mostly overcast sky with no moon helped hide *Batfish* while on the surface. In addition, he attacked from the east on the first two attacks as that direction provided the least contrast between sky and horizon. However, Fyfe attacked at radar depth during the third attack because *Batfish* was to the west of the Japanese submarine and did not have the darker background as they did on the two previous attacks. Furthermore, on all three attacks, Fyfe utilized the minimum silhouette method to further help reduce the submarines visibility and to help keep torpedo gyro angles close to zero. These tactics seemed to work well as the attack by *Archerfish* on 14 February employed the same tactics: a night surface attack using radar and employing the minimum silhouette method.

General William "Billy" Mitchell's quote "The best defense against submarines is other submarines" should be modified. A submarine geared for the defensive role would be a coastal-type submarine or possibly one from the inter-war years, whose role was fleet support. Mitchell's quote modified says, "The best *offense* against submarines is other submarines." The submarine was built as a weapon of war, and although ideally suited for commerce raiding, with an aggressive skipper in command, like LCDR John K. Fyfe, *Batfish* proved its worth, and the worth of the fleet submarine, in conducting anti-submarine warfare missions

Chapter 5: Mistaken Identity

At approximately two minutes past midnight on February 10, 1945, LCDR John K. Fyfe, skipper of the *Batfish* was in the waters north of the Philippine Islands, making a surfaced torpedo attack on an Imperial Japanese Navy submarine. On February 11, just a few minutes past 10 PM, Fyfe attacked a second Japanese submarine identified as *RO-112* and on February 13, just before 5 AM he attacked a third Japanese submarine identified as *RO-113*. These attacks happened within a seventy-six hour time span. Controversy has surrounded the identity of the first submarine almost since the day of the sinking.

By the end of January 1945, Japan decided to pull back the Japanese Air Force from the Philippines and operate from bases in Formosa.[1] In February 1945, General Douglas MacArthur's forces dislodged the Imperial Army north of Manila and important Japanese officials wanted to escape from Luzon and the advancing Allied threat.[2] Code breakers picked up information that the Japanese intended to use submarines to ferry ammunition from Formosa to Luzon and then evacuate pilots from Luzon back to Formosa.[3] These same submarines would also transport plane crews from Batulinao and top-ranked personnel from Aparri, both in northern Luzon, to Formosa, in connection with the pullback.[4] An ULTRA intelligence intercept on February 6, 1945 indicated that the evacuation was underway.[5] Japan assigned four Japanese submarines (*RO-46, RO-112, RO-113*, and *RO-115*) to the evacuation mission.[6] Waiting patiently, deployed in positions along the anticipated routes of the Japanese submarines was a three-submarine wolf pack comprised of *Batfish, Archerfish*, and *Blackfish*.[7] As the Japanese were busy evacuating their personnel from Aparri, Fyfe, aware of the possibility of Japanese submarines in his area, patrolled the Baboyan Channel north of the Philippines, searching for the enemy.[8]

Fyfe, as reported in the official report of *Batfish's* sixth patrol, identifies the first Japanese submarine only as an "I" class submarine.[9] Officers of *Batfish* witnessed the destruction of this submarine, officially credited as *I-41*, however, different authors and historians have reached different conclusions as to which submarine Fyfe actually sank on February 10.[10] In addition to *I-41*, other Japanese submarines suggested include *RO-45*, *RO-46*, *RO-55*, and *RO-115*. Some sources state that additional Japanese submarines were not lost at this time suggesting that the claimed sinking was either a failed attack on a submarine sunk later or a premature explosion of a previously fired torpedo.[11] Evidence shows Fyfe definitely sank a submarine at this time; the issue is determining which submarine.

Some claims suggest that the four evacuation submarines consisted of *RO-45*, *RO-55*, *RO-112* and *RO-113*.[12] As will be shown, *RO-45* was lost prior to February 1945. The main confusion centers on *RO-55* and *RO-115* as both patrolled in the same general vicinity west of Luzon at approximately the same time in early February 1945. The confusion and misidentification between *RO-55* and *RO-115* has prevented a clear-cut candidate for the first submarine sunk by Fyfe in February 1945.[13]

Even after more than sixty-six years, there is still speculation as to which Japanese submarine Fyfe sank on February 10, 1945. Japanese records, which most early historians accepted at face value, support *I-41*. A few authors claim Fyfe's first victim was *RO-55*, others *RO-115*, and still others leave the question in doubt.[14] Even with overwhelming evidence to the contrary, some claim that the only Japanese submarines lost at this time were the two officially credited to Fyfe and *Batfish*: *RO-112* and *RO-113*. Orita and Harrington concluded, "I think American crewmen interpreted a premature explosion as a hit. We lost no other boats in that area at that time."[15] This statement is clearly in error as two Japanese Monographs plainly state *RO-115* was lost in this area and at this time.[16] To add to the confusion, the Tabular Record of Movement (TROM) for *RO-55* makes the following statement: "Some sources claim the RO-55 was sunk on 10 February 1945 in the Luzon Strait by the USS BATFISH (SS-310), but, most probably, this was the RO-115."[17] However, when reading the TROM for *RO-115*, the same authors indicate surface vessels sank *RO-115* 31 January.[18] Even Japanese authors disagree on how and when *RO-115* sank. Orita and Harrington agree that surface ships caused the demise of *RO-115*.[19] Hashimoto claims *RO-115* was the victim of Fyfe's first torpedo attack.[20] Recent work indicates the first submarine sunk by Fyfe was *RO-115*.[21] Utilizing eyewitness descriptions, comparing Japanese and United States accounts, and applying a little deducting reasoning will reveal the identity of the Fyfe's first submarine sunk on February 10, 1945.

The AN/APR-1 radar detector, installed on U.S. submarines during World War II, was a broadband high-frequency receiver listening for the typical patterns of radar transmissions. Radar could be characterized by the frequency (or wavelength) of its carrier wave, Pulse Repetition Frequency (PRF) which is the number of times a second the radar wave pulses on and off, and pulse width.[22] On the evening of February 9, 1945, *Batfish's* SJ radar made contact with a Japanese submarine at a range of approximately 11,000 yards. Soon, the AN/APR-1 radar detector picked up foreign radar emissions coming from the Japanese submarine.[23] After a failed first attack on the Japanese submarine, Fyfe closed into visual range and attacked a second time. The resulting explosion and the cessation of radar emissions, as recorded in the patrol log (Appendix 1), verified the destruction of the Japanese submarine.[24]

There were two definite attacks on this Japanese submarine. During the first attack, Fyfe fired four torpedoes at the target. All torpedoes missed due to an error in the estimated speed of the enemy submarine as tracking party estimated the target was traveling at twelve knots when instead it was fourteen knots. Three torpedoes during the second attack produced one hit that destroyed the Japanese submarine. Fyfe noted in his patrol report the following observation:

> "Damage determined by: Saw one torpedo hit from a range of 900 yards. Target exploded with a brilliant red flame and sank almost immediately leaving a large oil slick that extended over a radius of two miles. Target could be seen blowing apart on radar screen." [25]

Additional attacks on subsequent days resulting in sinking Japanese submarines *RO-112* and *RO-113*. We can conclude that the first attack was not a failed attack on an enemy sunk later nor was it a premature explosion of a previously fired torpedo. Fyfe's vivid description does not support either position. He and the *Batfish* crew tracked this submarine, received radar emissions from it, visually identified it, witnessed its destruction, noted the cessation of radar emissions after the torpedo attack and then noted the diesel smell and heavy oil slick. This confirms that Fyfe, between

February 9 and 13, 1945, destroyed three, and not two, different Japanese submarines.

Eyewitness accounts of the attack on the first submarine only identified it as an "I" class submarine. *Batfish* bridge crew saw the enemy submarine during the attack, but it was too dark to tell if it was an I-boat or an RO-boat.[26] Interestingly, in the patrol report, Fyfe also describes the *RO-112* and *RO-113* as "I" class submarines, suggesting that all three Japanese submarines were of the same approximate size and configuration.[27] The difference should have been obvious if the first submarine was an "I" class submarine. The "I" class submarine is 148 feet longer and 1,795 tons heavier than a standard RO-100 class submarine.[28] With Fyfe calling all three submarines "I" class subs, then their size and configuration must have been comparable. So the question remains, which submarine was it? The best way to determine the answer is by the process of elimination from the list of the five suggested Japanese submarines.

As already mentioned, official Japanese sources indicate that the first submarine sunk was *I-41*.[29] Some authors have agreed with this designation from the end of the war until recently.[30,31] Others contradict this, stating a coordinated attack by USS *Lawrence C. Taylor* (DE-415), USS *Melvin R. Nawman* (DE-416) and aircraft from USS *Anzio* (CVE-57) sank *I-41* at 6:30 AM on November 18, 1944 at 12-44 N, 130-42E, east of Samar.[32] This would place the sinking of *I-41* more than two months before *Batfish's* February 10 attack.

Some authors incorrectly suggest *RO-45* as the first submarine sunk.[33] *RO-45* was not part of the evacuation force and furthermore the USS *MacDonough* (DD-351) and USS *Stephen Potter* (DD-538) sank *RO-45* on April 30, 1944 sixty-five miles south-southwest of the island of Truk (06-13N, 151-19E).[34] This would be almost ten months prior to the *Batfish* attack.

RO-46 did make one evacuation trip when it departed Takao, Formosa on February 7, 1945 to rescue stranded pilots from Batulinao in northern Luzon.[35] *RO-46* successfully disembarked the passengers at Takao on February 12 and then departed for the Japanese homeland.[36] Aircraft from USS *Tulagi* (CVE-72) reported sinking *RO-46* on April 29, 1945 more than two months after the *Batfish* attack.[37]

The identification issue lies mainly between the two remaining submarines, *RO-55* and *RO-115*. The following discussion illustrates some of the confusion surrounding these two submarines. Morison incorrectly identified *RO-115* as another submarine, attacking the transport ship USS

Cavalier (APA-37) on January 30, 1945.[38] The submarine that actually made the attack on the *Cavalier* was *RO-46.*[39] This goes to show that misidentification in the historical literature exists. To complicate the issue, both *RO-55* and *RO-115* were scheduled to patrol in the same general area, west to northwest of Luzon, at the same time and both submarines disappeared within a week of each other. Adding more confusion to the issue, there are three dates where U.S. naval forces sank Japanese submarines: January 31, February 7 and February 10. Therefore, we need a more detailed examination of these two submarines.

RO-55, scheduled to arrive on patrol in the Mindoro-Manila area on February 5, disappeared in early February 1945, somewhere west of Luzon. (Figure 5.1). On February 2, *RO-55* reported that enemy aircraft attacked the submarine and indicated there would be a delay in reaching its patrol area west of Mindoro by five days. This was the last report from the *RO-55.*[40] However, five days later on February 7, Hackett and Kingsepp claim *RO-55* attacked a convoy headed for Leyte Gulf.[41] *Thomason* (DE 203) picked up the surfaced submarine on radar and the submarine submerged as the destroyer escort approached. *Thomason* then attacked with Mark 10 "hedgehog" projector charges and presumably sunk *RO-55* at 11:30 PM on February 7, 1945 at 15-27N, 119-25E, off Iba, Luzon, Philippines.[42] This falls within *RO-55's* patrol area. Morison suggests that *RO-55* escaped the February 7 attack, only to be the first of three submarines sunk two days later by Fyfe in *Batfish.*[43] This is doubtful, as the submarine, more than likely the *RO-55*, did not survive the *Thomason* attack.[44]

Historians disagree upon the time and place of *RO-115's* sinking. Like the *RO-55*, some indicate the sinking was the result of attacks by surface ships west of Luzon.[45] Others claim *RO-115* was the first submarine sunk by Fyfe north of Luzon.[46] A few credit *RO-115's* sinking to surface ships on January 31, 1945 (15-03N, 119-07E). The Japanese Navy officially listed *RO-115* as presumed lost on February 21, 1945.[47] On February 2, 1945, two days after *RO-115's* alleged sinking and the same day aircraft attacked *RO-55*, *RO-115* was given orders to leave her patrol area west of Manila, which was the same general area that *RO-55* was to patrol five days later on February 7. *RO-115's* orders were to proceed north and take part in evacuation operations; however, whether the submarine received these orders is unknown. Were these orders received by *RO-115* or was the submarine destroyed en route on January 31, 1945?[48]

When examining the locations where *RO-55* was sunk and where the January 31 attack took place, both are north of *RO-115's* patrol zone west

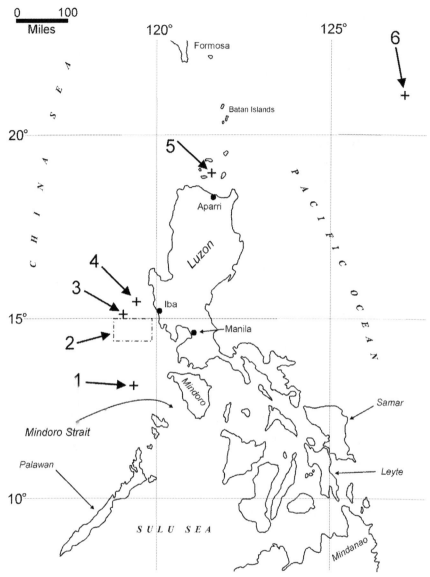

Figure 5.1. Japanese submarine sinking locations. 1) January 31 1945 attack location based on Tabular Record of Movement (Hackett and Kingsepp), 2) location of *RO-115's* patrol area, 3) January 31, 1945 attack location based on deck log from USS *Moore* (DD442), 4) February 7, 1945 attack location of *RO-55*, 5) February 9-10, 1945 attack location by *Batfish*, 6) February 14, 1945 attack location by *Archerfish*.

of Manila (Figure 5.1). It would seem that *RO-115* was not in the attack area until at least February 2. Apparently, *RO-115* had left the area three days prior to the sinking of *RO-55*. The arrival of this estimated positioning is explained shortly, but first an examination of the January 31 attack is needed.

The events of January 31, 1945 contribute to a majority of the discrepancy as this is the date several authors suggest U.S. surface forces sank *RO-115*. The United States destroyers *Bell* (DD-587), *O'Bannon* (DD450), *Jenkins* (DD-447) and *Moore* (DE-442) were operating to the west of Luzon in an attempt to intercept Japanese transports. Just before 8 PM, the light cruiser USS *Boise* (CL-47) made radar contact on a surfaced vessel. *Bell* also picked up the contact and, along with *O'Bannon*, was detached to investigate. The radar contact apparently submerged as the two destroyers approached. The ships made sonar contact and the two destroyers dropped a few depth charges but soon lost contact with the submarine. *Bell* reacquired contact and dropped another round of depth charges as *Moore* joined the attack. An oil slick soon appeared on the ocean surface and at approximately 9:30 PM, *Moore* launched five Mark 10 "hedgehog" charges over the oil slick and apparently sank the unidentified submarine at location 13-20N, 119-20E.[49] The attacking ships heard and felt an underwater explosion shortly after midnight at which time they assumed sank the submarine.[50] The full event, including the description of the destruction of this submarine, is illustrated in an excerpt from the deck log from *Moore* presented in Appendix 4.[51]

Adding to the overall confusion is that of the two different locations for the January 31 attack. Hackett and Kingsepp state that the January 31 attack by *Moore* took place at location 13-20N, 119-20E.[52] However, the deck log from the *Moore* claims the attack location was at 15-03N, 119-07E.[53] These two locations are almost one hundred miles apart (Locations 1 and 3 on Figure 5.1). The attack could not have happened at two locations, therefore *Moore's* deck log will be accepted as the official location, placing this attack near the February 7 *RO-55* attack and north of *RO-115's* patrol area, west of Manila.

With the exception of *RO-115*, there is no report of any other U.S. surface forces attacking and sinking a Japanese submarine at this time and location; furthermore, Japanese records do not indicate that any other Japanese submarine was in the vicinity of this attack. However, this may be the norm and not the exception. *Archerfish* had a similar event happen on February 14, 1945 when she encountered and sank an unidentified Japanese submarine. Official documents and Japanese sources do not give *Archerfish* credit for this sinking, but by examining an excerpt from the patrol report in Appendix 5, and the precise details contained within, it is clear that *Archerfish* tracked and sank an enemy submarine.[54]

How does the *Archerfish* attack apply to the attack of January 31, 1945? *Archerfish* tracked, identified and witnessed the violent destruction of an enemy submarine. Japanese records give no indication of any submarine being lost near the *Archerfish* attack. However, the vivid description of the target indicates otherwise and it is clear that the *Archerfish* sank an unknown Japanese submarine of which there is no official record. In applying this to the January 31 attack, could there have been another, unknown submarine, similar to the *Archerfish* example, lurking in the waters that night and was it this unknown submarine that was sunk and not *RO-115*? As will be shown, the mostly likely explanation is that there were at least three submarines in the general vicinity west of Luzon in early February 1945: *RO-55*, *RO-115* and an unknown submarine. Determining which one of these submarines was lost on January 31 will reveal the identity of the submarine Fyfe san a few days later. Of the three most likely candidates, we can eliminate *RO-55* because as previously shown, surface ships sank it on February 7 in its patrol area. This leaves *RO-115* and a possible unknown submarine, but a few questions remain.

Was the submarine in the January 31 attack the *RO-115*? To answer this question, we need to know the location of *RO-115*. An RO-100 class submarine had an endurance of 1,000 miles at twelve knots.[55] The trip from Singapore to *RO-115's* patrol zone west of Manila would take almost four days at an assumed speed of twelve knots, with one required stop for fuel (it was over a 1,200-mile trip from Singapore to *RO-115's* patrol zone). Hackett and Kingsepp state *RO-115* left Singapore on January 22, 1945, and headed northeastward to patrol the area west of Luzon and that it was not heard from again.[56] Japanese Monograph 184 claims *RO-115* left Singapore on January 25 for the waters west of Luzon.[57] This would place *RO-115* in its patrol area sometime between January 26 and January 31, depending on which departure date, January 22 or January 25, is correct. Again, we will take the official document as the accepted date. The January 31 attack occurred northwest of the Mindoro Straits, approximately 130 miles to the west-northwest of Mindoro. At the time of this attack, *RO-115* would have most likely been in its patrol area off the west coast of Luzon (west of Manila) putting it south of the January 31 attack by a <u>minimum</u> of fifteen miles and even further from the location where surface ships sank *RO-55* on February 7. On the outside chance that *RO-115* was the target of January 31 attack, did it survive only to fall victim to Fyfe a few days later? *Moore's* deck log excerpt indicates that the submarine attacked on January 31 did not survive the attack based on the presence of an oil slick, debris and the underwater explosion. If we continue to assume that the January 31 target was *RO-115* and if it did not survive the attack, what submarine did Fyfe attack and sink on February 10?

Examining the facts we have, we know that when Fyfe made both of his attacks on the first submarine, the target was sailing northward with an observed course varying between 309° and 020°. Based on the location of these attacks, this would put the Japanese submarine on a direct line between Aparri on northern Luzon and the southern end of Formosa. The evacuation submarines would follow this approximate route. The significance of this is that, of the four submarines assigned to evacuation duties, the only possible submarine that it could have been was *RO-115* as Fyfe sank *RO-112* and *RO-113* on the following nights and *RO-46* made a successful evacuation run on February 12.

On February 2, naval leaders ordered *RO-115* to Takao. Six days later, *RO-115* was heading north in the direction of Formosa from northern Luzon at the time of Fyfe's attack. The only issue with this hypothesis is that the evacuation submarines were to first head to Takao, Formosa, load supplies and ammunition, then sail to northern Luzon. Japanese records do not indicate if, or why, *RO-115* headed for northern Luzon first before heading north to Takao. There are intangibles that cannot be answered, so estimated guesses are required. First, there was an issue of fuel. Japanese Monograph 95 claims the evacuation submarines were at the "limit of their serviceability", which probably refers to fuel.[58] *RO-115* had sailed from Singapore and would have needed to fuel at least once en route to its patrol zone. The submarine would have been in its patrol zone for 4+ days before sailing northward to Formosa. A reduction of speed from a cruising speed of twelve knots to something slower would help conserve fuel and would explain the length of time to reach the area of Fyfe's attack. Japanese Monograph 95 also states that *RO-46* was the only submarine to perform its duties.[59] However, what does "perform" mean? Could this mean that *RO-115* did not make an evacuation attempt? Does it mean that *RO-115* did evacuate personnel from north Luzon but did not reach its destination? Why was *RO-115* in the "evacuation slot" if it did not attempt an evacuation run? One possibility is that the orders required *RO-115* to be in a "safe" zone that may have been the line between northern Luzon and Formosa. Another possibility is that *RO-115* stopped somewhere on northern Luzon to refuel, being at its limit of serviceability, before heading to Formosa. A likely explanation is that *RO-115* did stop for fuel in northern Luzon and possibly took on passengers before heading north to Formosa. This question can probably never be answered, but regardless, for whatever reason, *RO-115* was north of Aparri heading north on the night of February 10. The following paragraph brings to light an observation that helps verify this claim and helps identify the first submarine Fyfe sank.

A key piece of the puzzle lies in the radar emissions given off by all three of the submarines Fyfe sank. The patrol report indicates that all three Japanese submarines were emitting a radar signal of 157-158 megacycles and a PRF of 500. Only three radar models were in use on surface ships and submarines at the end of the war: Type 3 Mark 1 Model 3 and Type 2 Mark 2 Model 1 for air search and the Mark 2 Model 2 for surface search.[60] Additionally, only three classes of Japanese submarines had radar: the I-400 class, the I-10 class and the RO-100 class. The RO-100 class, which included the *RO-112*, *RO-113* and *RO-115*, had the Type 3 Mark 1 Model 3 radar that for submarines was anti-air radar.[61] This model transmitted at 150 megacycles with a PRF of 500.[62] All three submarines Fyfe sank transmitted at approximately 150 mgcs and a PRF of 500. Therefore, these submarines were all RO-100 class submarines that clearly rules out *RO-55* as a potential target as it was not equipped with this radar. Interestingly, Carpenter and Polmar indicate five classes of Japanese submarines had radar installed: I-1, I-10, I-14, RO-100 and I-400.[63] Later, when describing submarine losses, they discuss the *Batfish* incident where they claim the first submarine was *RO-55*:

> All three BATFISH successes came through the detection of radar emissions from the Japanese submarines. The Japanese submarine, the *RO-55*, appears to have used her air-search radar continuously, apprehensive of a surprise attack.[64]

The question is if the only "RO" class submarine to have radar was the RO-100 class, how was *RO-55* using air-search radar if it was not installed on that class of submarine? The answer is that the submarine Fyfe sank was a class of submarine with radar installed; either one of the previously listed I-class or RO-100 class boats, again ruling out *RO-55*. The submarine that Fyfe attacked was in the right place and heading in the right direction to coincide with the evacuation events previously outlined. Other than one of the four Japanese submarines designated for the evacuation runs, there should not have been any other Japanese submarines in the area of the *Batfish* attack. That the victim of the January 31 attack could have been *RO-115* is extremely doubtful due to *RO-115* being in its assigned patrol area approximately fifteen to one hundred miles to the south of the attack location on January 31.

If the January 31 victim was not *RO-115*, what submarine did U.S. surface forces attack? As stated previously, Japanese records report no other submarine west of Luzon on January 31, but as we saw, neither did they report one near the *Archerfish* attack. Interestingly, there were several smaller HA-class Japanese submarines operating in the waters west of the Philippines in January and February of 1945, including the *HA-69, HA-76, HA-81, HA-82* and *HA-84*, patrolling either off the islands Cebu and Mindanao or in the Mindoro Strait. *HA-76, HA-81* and *HA-84* made attacks in the Mindoro Strait on January 24-25, 1945, putting them less than 100 miles from the location of the January 31, 1945 attack. After January, there is no additional reported activity for either *HA-76* or *HA-81*.[65] With these two submarines operating in the area and then no further information concerning their activities after the reported attack on January 31 it is possible that the unidentified submarine attacked by surface vessels was either *HA-76* or *HA-81*. It is important to note that the only contact was by radar and by sonar. U.S. surface forces never visually identified the submarine sunk on January 31, neither could they ascertain size, speed, type and direction of travel. The submarine attacked on January 31 and sunk by surface vessels was more than likely an unknown submarine, possibly the *HA-76* or *HA-81*, and not *RO-115*.

Based on available information, Fyfe's first submarine was *RO-115*. Supporting evidence includes 1) surface ships sank *I-41* several months earlier; 2) surface forces sank *RO-45* almost a year earlier than the *Batfish* attack; 3) after a successful evacuation run, surface forces sank *RO-46* two months after the *Batfish* attack; 4) surface ships sank *RO-55* on February 7, 1945 off the western coast of Luzon. In addition, this submarine was not part of the evacuation operation and never received orders to participate in the evacuation detail; 5) Fyfe's comments in the patrol log (i.e. the vivid description of the tracking, attack, and destruction of the Japanese submarine) refute any statement of a premature torpedo explosion. In addition, Fyfe reported that the radar emissions ceased abruptly and that the submarine screws stopped immediately after the attack. There is also the strong diesel smell and heavy oil slick encountered right after the attack; 6) in the patrol report, the night of February 9 was dark and by the crew's own admission, it was too dark to distinguish the class of submarine on the first attack. Fyfe described all three Japanese submarines as "I" class boats; however, the second and third submarines were RO-100 class submarines. If the second and third submarines, initially identified as I-class boats, turned out to be RO-100 class boats, then the first submarine was also an RO-100 class boat. They were apparently all the same approximate size and configuration and as previously shown, the size and tonnage differences between an "I" and RO-100 class submarine are very distinct; 7) The RO-100 class Japanese submarines were one of three classes of submarines equipped with air search radar (Type 3 Mark 1 Module 3). The other two classes were the I-10 and the I-400. Both of these classes of submarines were significantly larger then the RO-100 class. The RO-100 submarines broadcast at 150 mgcs with 500 PRF. All three submarines transmitted at 157-158 mgcs and 500 PRF. With the first submarine transmitting at that range, it is impossible for the first victim to be the *RO-55*, as that class of submarine did not have radar installed. It could not have been one of the I-class boats as there are no records of any of them being in the vicinity of the attack. The first submarine was an RO-100 class submarine and there were no others in the vicinity but *RO-115*.

RO-115 was one of four submarines scheduled for evacuation duty. Fyfe sank the *RO-112* and *RO-113* on following nights. U.S. surface forces sank the other evacuation submarine, *RO-46*, later in the war. The only remaining candidate is *RO-115* that was en route from its patrol area off Manila northward to Formosa by way of northern Luzon, when on the night of February 9, 1945 Fyfe and *Batfish* intercepted and sank it. The submarine attacked and sunk on January 31, 1945 by *Bell* and *Moore* was not *RO-115*. It could have been an unknown Japanese submarine operating in the area or it likely was either *HA-76* or *HA-81*, two of several smaller HA-class submarines reported to be operating in the same general vicinity as the January 31, 1945 attack. The only clear-cut candidate for the first submarine Fyfe sank is *RO-115*.

Chapter 6: Salvation

During World War II, eighty-six U.S. submarines rescued 504 aviators of Army, Navy, Marine, Australian and British forces.[1] Admiral Lockwood strategically placed submarines, referred to as the "Lifeguard League", to rescue carrier planes or bomber crews forced to ditch in the open sea. Although *Batfish* did not set any records for aviators rescued, the submarine did perform one rescue operation in July 1945. And for three Army aviators who managed to escape their damaged B-25 bomber, *Batfish* was the most important submarine in the world.

A military aviator's life was worth taking trouble to preserve. A trained and seasoned pilot represented a huge capital investment and the Navy could not easily replace him.[2] When aviators ditched their planes, Admiral Charles Lockwood, Commander Submarines Pacific, wanted them to know that a submarine was going to do everything in its power to find them. The boost to the morale of the pilots was quite noticeable.[3] LCDR Walter L. Small, skipper of *Batfish* on its seventh patrol, was able to demonstrate this when anti-aircraft fire hit a B-25 bomber returning from a bombing mission on the Japanese homeland's southernmost island on its way out from the target. The bomber ditched in the ocean, exploding on impact. The impact threw three crewmembers from the plane; the other three crewmembers were lost in the ditching.[4] This is their story.

The Navy classified the submarine as an effective offensive weapon of naval warfare. Its primary assigned mission was to sink and destroy enemy vessels. Therefore, the Navy usually declined utility assignments to serve the missions of other forces, with the exception of reconnaissance, as an unjustified employment of a valuable offensive weapon of war.[5] The Japanese had used submarines as lifeguards since the opening days of the war, but until the Americans began launching aggressive carrier operations, lifeguard roles for U.S. submarines did not get much attention.[6] Late in the summer of 1943, shortly before the Tarawa invasion, there came into being the so-called "Lifeguard League", which would become the largest of the special submarine operations.[7]

Lifeguard missions required submarines to stand off enemy islands during carrier air strikes to pick up U.S. pilots forced to ditch.[8] Lifeguard submarines had to operate on the surface, usually in dangerous locations close to Japanese shore-based installations or airfields.[9] In addition, there was also the risk of accidental attack by friendly ships and planes.[10] *Snook* (SS 279) and *Steelhead* (SS 280) performed the first lifeguard missions in September 1943 during carrier raids on the Marcus and Gilbert Islands, respectively; however, no planes ditched.[11] *Skate* (SS 305) performed the first successful lifeguard mission on October 7, 1943 rescuing six downed aviators off Wake Island.[12]

As the number of U.S. submarines increased in the Pacific towards the later part of World War II, lifeguard operations operated out of two locations: Iwo Jima and Okinawa. As each submarine group needed an individual title, the Navy dropped the term "Lifeguard League" and designated the lifeguard group for Okinawa planes as the "Texas League" and the group for Marianas planes as the "National League."[13] Additionally, each group organized special combat air patrols to protect submarines during rescues. The air patrol helped locate downed fliers, defend surfaced submarines, and guide ditching aircraft to the submarines vicinity.[14]

From late 1944 through 1945, lifeguard missions occupied part of the time of practically every submarine sent to patrol around Japan. Submarines continued to provide air rescue services for carrier planes, but lifeguard missions now included B-29 strikes into Japan.[15] *Tang* (SS 306) holds the record for the most aviators rescued on a single patrol with twenty-two as it performed lifeguard duty off Truk Atoll on April 30, 1944. *Tigrone* (SS 419) holds the record for the most rescues during the war with thirty-one. Submarines picked up seven aviators in 1943, 117 in 1944 and 380 in 1945. Altogether, U.S. submarines saved 504 U.S. aviators from capture or drowning during World War II.[16]

On June 26, 1945, *Batfish* departed the Submarine Base at Pearl Harbor, en route to Saipan, in compliance with ComSubPacAdCom Op Order 123-A-45. Small conducted daily training dives and drills until July 8 when at approximately 10:30 AM, *Batfish* reached Saipan and moored alongside the Fulton-Class submarine tender USS *Orion* (AS 18) for voyage repairs.[17]

After repairs were completed, *Batfish* got underway on July 10 at approximately 2:00 PM for lifeguard duty, under escort of *LCI222* in compliance with ComSubPac Op Order No. 153-45. The first report of a downed aviator came in at 3:32 PM on July 16 when *Batfish* received a message of a man in rubber boat. Small sent a message that he would get him; however, the plane circling the downed aviator replied that *Argonaut* (SS 475) was also heading in that direction. At 5:25 PM, *Batfish* lookouts sighted *Argonaut* recovering the aviator. Two days later on July 18, at approximately 1:00 AM, *Batfish* received a message of eight parachutes sighted off the China coast, almost 250 miles from *Batfish's* position. Knowing that there were up to three other submarines closer to that position, Small decided not to attempt a rescue.

Batfish surfaced at 9:15 AM on July 19 for lifeguard duty. After not seeing any planes for over an hour, and knowing that the strike was to end at 10:30 AM, Small assumed that command canceled the strike because of a typhoon near Okinawa. On July 20, there was still no message from Okinawa as a typhoon was still probably in that vicinity so Small assumed that command either cancelled or postponed the strike and he decided to patrol in close to shore. The same type of events happened for the next several days as *Batfish* performing lifeguard duties. Whether messages were not being sent or they were not receiving them was unknown so Small had a message sent asking if they had missed something. Okinawa responded that they had not missed anything. Small, with apparent frustration, noted in the patrol report:

> It would certainly help if we could get the dope on days that there are no strikes so that we would feel free to patrol. As it is we can't get far enough away from our lifeguard station to feel that we are actually patrolling. We have been lifeguarding for ten days now and not an air strike yet.[18]

Come to find out, on July 20 *Batfish* lookouts sighted a PBM and eight P-51 Mustangs. *Batfish* established communication with they aircraft and Small discovered that the planes were the submarines air cover for a strike that was just beginning. To his surprise, Small learned that there had been about five to seven strikes in the last ten days and there had been no information on any except those cancelled on July 19 and July 23. However, the situation was about to change for Small and *Batfish*.

On July 28, 2nd Lt. Robert Bleicher and 1st Lt. James Van Epps attended a briefing, informing them they would be serving as co-pilot and navigator-bombardier, respectively, in a B-25J Mitchell Bomber, piloted by Captain Nathan Mangeno (820th Squadron, 41st Bomber Group). Other members of Mangeno's crew included SSgt. Joe J. Kinkley (Engineer/Gunner), SSgt. Frederick V. Force, Jr. (Armorer/Gunner) and Cpl. Thomas E. Billings (Radio/Gunner).[19] The North American B-25 Mitchell was a twin-engine bomber that became standard equipment for the Allied Air Forces in World War II. It was perhaps the most versatile aircraft of the war as it was the most heavily armed airplane in the world, was used for high- and low-level bombing, strafing, photoreconnaissance, and submarine patrol.[20]

The final briefing came on the morning of July 29 when the bomber crew received their target (Figure 6.1). The mission was a low-level bomb run on a railroad bridge on the island of Miyazaki, Kyushu, Japan.[21] The crew left Okinawa around mid-morning on its 650-mile, three-plus hour flight.[22] The flight would follow the path of Okinawa to Yaku Shima to target and then back to Okinawa.[23]

Mangeno's B-25J was in the number three position on flight leader Dan Hill's left wing.[24] Around noon on the 29th, the bombers approached the eastern shore of Kyushu and began their run on the railroad bridge.

> As the squadron began going up the river valley toward the bridge, the formation kept feathering out wider. We were on Capt. Dan Hill's left wing, and we were to be forced completely out of the line on the bridge. I saw a town, and we were headed much more over the center of it than the main group that was going up the river. Regardless, we dropped our bombs from a very low altitude of 500 feet.[25]

Intelligence reports indicated that the target defenses would be light. Intelligence was misinformed.[26] Mangeno's B-25J took a hit going out to sea away from the target.[27] Anti-aircraft fire hit the plane in the left wing fuel tank between the engine and the fuselage.[28] Shortly thereafter, tail gunner SSgt. Force reported being injured in the right thigh and hip from flak.[29] As Mangeno tried to gain some altitude, he received a damage report that there was smoke coming from the left wing.[30]

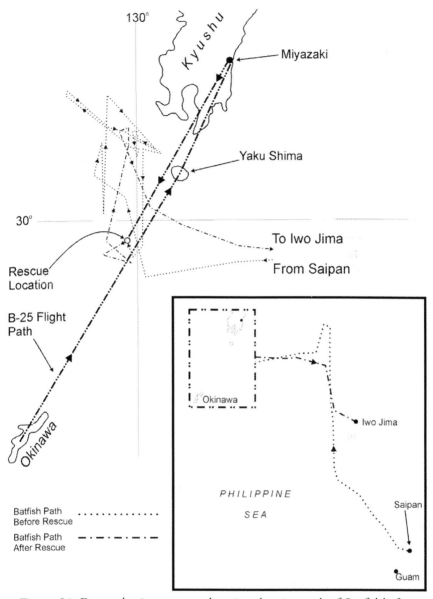

Figure 6.1. Downed aviators rescue location showing path of *Batfish* before and after rescue and the B-25 flight path to and way from the target at Miyazaki.

As the B-25J reached an altitude of 4,000 feet, the rear crew members, along with Van Epps who had crawled across the tight space over the bomb bay connecting the front and rear areas, treated SSgt. Force as best as they could.[31] The crew discussed the chances of bailing out since there were life rafts available, but they quickly vetoed that idea due to the injured tail gunner who could not parachute. Therefore, Mangeno decided to try and "ditch" the bomber.[32]

Mangeno gained some altitude and increased their speed for several minutes, hoping the fire might burn out. However, a report from the turret gunner was not good. There was limited visibility into the inside of the wing and the report was that there was increasing evidence of more fire inside the wing, which was affecting the wing structure itself.[33] Flight leader Dan Hill had stayed with the damaged plane the whole time and was reporting that the fire appeared to be out of control.[34] The crew prepared for ditching and dropped back down closer to the water. From high up, the ocean surface looked smooth, but as the bomber got closer, the "waves looked like mountains."[35]

As the bomber neared the water, Bleicher estimated the waves at ten feet high. Mangeno tried to align the plane with the troughs of water in the ocean.[36] The initial touch was smooth.[37] At approximately the same time, after what the pilot called a "severe bump" the right propeller came off the shaft and stayed about four feet ahead of the aircraft for a split second.[38] It seems that the "bump" caused the hydraulic system to burst as the landing gear came down and the plane exploded.[39] Regardless of the exact timing of these events, the bomber had become airborne again, only to re-enter the ocean at an angle between 35° and 40° nose down.[40] The bomber had disintegrated, with the rear fuselage separated from the wing assembly.[41]

Mangeno ditched the B-25J about eighty-five miles southwest of Kyushu near a small island in the Tokara Gunto. Mangeno, Bleicher and Van Epps were on the flight deck and were thrown clear from the bomber as it hit, going out the front of the plane. The three enlisted men, Kinkley, Force, and Billings, were in the radio compartment and were lost, not surviving the impact.[42] The cabin was gone; the rear fuselage was also gone. Fire and dense smoke heavily engulfed the wing.[43]

When Mangeno hit the water, he was still strapped to his steel seat and started sinking towards the bottom. He came to enough to release his seat harness but in doing so also released his seat pack with his one-man life raft. He still had his "Mae West" to inflate to bring him to the surface.[44]

As Bleicher came to the surface, he believed he was the sole survivor and, a mild panic came over him. He then heard voices and eventually saw two people about one hundred yards away, yelling for him to get away from the bomber.[45] He swam away from the plane and activated his "Mae West". Mangeno and Van Epps were struggling to inflate the one-man life raft as Bleicher approached. Within ten minutes or so, they got both remaining life rafts inflated, putting Mangeno into one of them and Van Epps, who was the more seriously injured, into the other.[46] They eventually got all three men into the two rafts.[47] A search commenced for the other crewmembers, but the three men were never located.[48]

All this time, flight leader Dan Hill had been circling the three men in the water as they tried to assess their injuries.[49] Mangeno felt as if his left leg was broken. Van Epps had pain in his left leg and when he reached down, all he could feel was bone. He thought he had lost his left foot. Actually, his leg was torn open from below the knee to the ankle. Bleicher only had minor cuts and bruises.[50] While Dan Hill had been circling, he had radioed in the ditching and requested Okinawa dispatch a rescue plane.[51]

At 3:15 PM on July 29, *Batfish* intercepted a message indicating that three men were in the water approximately ninety miles south of their position. Subsequent messages sounded like a PBM (or flying boat) would land and pick them up, but Small headed south at flank speed anyway. PBM's would fly "Dumbo" missions to rescue pilots and aircrew that had crashed into the sea. The missions were named after the popular Disney cartoon and the name stuck to the plane. PBM's relied on radar to find the downed plane, but there were times where everyone on board the airplane would be searching, as it was extremely hard to spot a life raft in the sea. Sometimes, PBM's would land and pick up the downed aviators, but often the seas were too rough. They would fly over them and waggle their wings; a signal to the aviators the PBM spotted them. Sometimes the PBM would drop a float light or a raft. Usually the "Dumbo" would just circle until a ship would come to pick them up. The circling often went on for hours, but that was one of the PBM's strengths. It could fly for fourteen hours or more. If a rescue ship still had not arrived before the PBM ran out of fuel, another PBM arrive to take up the vigil.[52]

After a while, a large, two-engine gull-wing seaplane, called a Navy Martin "Mariner" PBM arrived on station at which time Dan Hill departed for Okinawa. The aviators thought that they had a good chance of being picked up and maybe would be able to search for other survivors. The PBM made three landing attempts, aborting each one due to the very high seas.[53] The PBM instead dropped a large rubber raft that they were able to get to but had trouble inflating. Once they finally inflated the raft, they were able to get into it, but kept their one-man rafts close by.[54]

Some time had passed when a B-17 bomber headed toward the men and dropped a good-sized wooden boat by parachute. The boat drifted well beyond their position and once it hit the water they lost sight of it. They made an effort to paddle in the direction of the last sighting of the boat and parachutes, but with the rough sea, it was impossible for them to hold a heading.[55] A second B-17 appeared about ten minutes later, made a better drop and they were able to reach the boat. The boat stayed within their sight and the three men paddled for it.[56] When they finally got to the boat, the parachutes had filled with water and they had to get them released before he water-filled parachutes pulled the boat under. Normally there was a release mechanism that they would have been able to use but with the strain put on by the water, they would not release.[57] The three men attempted several times to knock out a king pin that was holding the chutes to the boat, but the parachutes filling with water created too much pressure on the pins. Using their knives, which they always carried with them, it took approximately fifteen minutes to cut all of the nylon lines.[58] The men finally made it inside the boat around 5:00 PM and had a chance to dry off, and take advantage of dry clothes and first aid supplies.[59]

The twenty-seven foot long boat, termed a "Flying Dutchman", carried enough provisions for a fifteen hundred mile voyage. It weighed about a ton and could carry three times that weight.[60] The men were able to exchange their torn and oil-soaked gear for dry clothes. With the medical kit, they tried to care for their injuries. Mangeno had a broken leg, broken finger and minor lacerations. Van Epps' leg had been severely torn on both sides. Bleicher was in the best shape with only some bumps and severe bruising.[61] Their air cover, a PBM, stayed with them until dark because they were still close to the island.[62] However, after sundown and around 8:00 PM, they could hear the engines of the PBM diminish as it left them.

Around 4:00 PM, *Batfish* received a message that a B-17 had dropped a life raft and that at approximately 6:00 PM received news that the men were in the boat but that the PBM could not land because of increasing wind and seas. Small again notified Okinawa of their intentions to pick up the downed aviators, and provided their ETA. At 7:45 PM, the "Dumbo" left the survivors due to low fuel. *Batfish* was still an hour and a half away, slowed by high wind and heavy seas. Fyfe radioed Okinawa, asking if there would be a relief "Dumbo" to orbit the survivors who had a light in the boat and flares. Okinawa replied in the negative. Small noted in his patrol report:

We do not know the situation on Okinawa and are not criticizing but at 1945 the survivors were definitely located with us 1 1/2 hours away. If this base could possibly have provided a plane to drop a couple of one hour flares for the boat to stay close to, three badly injured and shocked men would have been saved a cold, wet, miserable 12 hours in a boat with a 25 knot wind and force 5 sea.[63]

At 9:15 PM, *Batfish* arrived in the vicinity of the survivors and began searching by firing green flares every 8,000 yards. There were numerous SD contacts throughout the night. The weather was miserably rough, not quite yet a typhoon and the submarine was pitching and rolling. However, since the crew knew the men were in the raft, and they realized that they could be bleeding to death, Small persisted in the search.[64] At 10:10, *Batfish* pick up a signal believed to be a Gibson Girl (survival radio transmitter). Small got the bearing and headed west. After chasing the signal for almost forty miles, the submarine ended up two miles south of Akusaki Jima. As the submarine approached the island the signal increased in intensity until it saturated dial, then the signal was lost and was not heard again. Small deduced that the Japanese knew that a search was on and the signal was an intentional deception. Small returned to the vicinity of the downed aviators and continued the search throughout the night firing green flares every four miles.

As the three men in the boat were trying to rest, they started seeing flares, some time around midnight, but did not hear any sounds. They decided that since they did not know the source of the flares, and since they were not very far from the bombed target, it might be better to take their chances in daylight, so they decided not to send up any answering flares.[65] Meanwhile, Small continued searching into the early hours of July 30. At 2:45 AM, a passing friendly patrol plane assisted in the search for an hour with negative results.

When day broke around 4:30 AM, the men in the boat could see land off in the distance. This was Japanese territory and they became very concerned. Searching through the supplies in the boat, Bleicher found some navigation maps, tossed them to Van Epps, and asked him to give him a heading. Thirty minutes later, and after much effort, Bleicher finally got one engine of the Flying Dutchman started, allowing them to keep from drifting toward the hostile shore. They set their course and on one engine, tried to put some distance between them and the island.[66]

Around 7:40 AM, a PBM (code name Playmate 15) arrived on station to assist in the search and thirty minutes later, the PBM located the survivors. According to *Batfish's* patrol log, it was about 8:10 AM when they received the message that the PBM had located the downed aviators at which point Small headed in that direction. At this point, there is a time discrepancy as Bleicher indicates the time was closer to 10:00 AM:

> It was about 10:00 AM when we saw a Martin Mariner returning. They Navy plane was coming right at us just right on line. When it was two or three miles from us, it made a turn to the right. We were very disappointed and started to get the flare guns out. Then it made a turn to the left, and I immediately knew what was underway. They possibly had not seen us yet but they were activating a "square search".[67]

Come first light, Small began the "square search" pattern, starting outward from the last reported position.[68] In a square search, the plane and submarine covered a specific pattern that eventually would cover every part of the search area. On their second leg, the PBM spotted the downed aviators and with their site gun telegraphed to them in Morse code "S-T-O-P." Bleicher shut down the engine and thought the PBM would land and pick them up. However, the PBM did not land, but continued to circle them for the next thirty minutes to an hour.[69]

It was not too much longer until Bleicher spotted the conning tower of a submarine approaching them. At first, he did not know if it was friend or foe, maybe due to some mild shock of the past twelve hours. However, it only took him a moment to realize that had it been an enemy submarine, the Navy plane would have engaged it in some type of combat even with light machine gun fire.

As the submarine pulled closer, several crewmembers and officers started to wave at the aviators.[70] The submarine came along side the Flying Dutchman and two crewmembers dove into the water to secure a line to the raft to draw it closer to the submarine.[71] The small boat was bobbing a distance of about twelve feet and with the movement of the boat and the submarine, requiring both parties carefully plan the exit from the small craft onto the submarine deck.[72] Bleicher was the first to exit the small boat, followed by Van Epps and then Mangeno. The first question they were asked was "Why didn't you answer our flares last night? We had steaks fixed for you".[73] *Batfish* crewmembers lowered all three men down the forward escape hatch, into the forward torpedo room. The patrol report outlines the rescue:

> At approximately 9:30 AM, at position Latitude 29° 28' N., Longitude 129° 53' E., 1st Lieut. Nathan Mangeno, 0-755384; 1st Lieut. James L. Van Epps, 0-702509; and 2nd Lieut. Robert L. Bleicher, 0-833296 of U.S. Army 41st Bomber Group, Squadron 820, Plane 879 were pulled from their life raft. Mangeno had fractured or broken his ankle and had a cut tendon in left middle finger. Van Epps had an eight inch long and four inch wide laceration to the bone in his left shin and also had two other bad, but lesser lacerations. Bleicher had a sprained back. All three had numerous minor lacerations and bruises and were suffering from shock and exposure. The three survivors stated that they did not believe the other three crew members got out of plane as it was on fire, and broke up when it hit the water at 125 knots.[74]

In spite of the highs seas, the crew of *Batfish*, in the span of about twenty minutes, got the three aviators aboard and then destroyed the small boat with gunfire.[75] Batfish's pharmacists mate treated the aviators for their injuries and stabilized Van Epps' leg. All three aviators received a liberal ration of "depth charge" whiskey to relax and help warm them up.[76] Mangeno, Bleicher and Van Epps anticipated a trip somewhere with a hospital, but to their surprise, Small told them the submarine would remain in their assigned area until they had permission to leave.[77] *Batfish* headed for station and its assigned patrol area to continue lifeguard duty until relieved.

Once on board, the first bunks assigned to the aviators were over the torpedoes in the forward torpedo room. Eventually the three received bunks in the officer's area, just aft of the forward torpedo room.[78] *Batfish* lookouts continued to see many friendly planes throughout the day. At about 1:45 PM, *Batfish* received a report of a fighter plane that had ditched and Small headed for its position only to find out about twenty-five minutes later that the pilot was definitely dead. Forty-five minutes later *Batfish* received another report of a downed plane; so once again, Small headed south to its position. After a six-hour search that included three to five planes, no survivors were located. Small did not proceed further as the reported position was over the line in air surface zone. Small made a trim dive and then at 7:50 PM, surfaced and headed north.

Friendly air and surface forces some times attacked submarines on lifeguard duty, in spite of all the precautions.[79] On August 1, 1945, *Batfish*, south of Kyushu was on the surface performing lifeguard duties when an Army B-25 turned and challenged her with a signal light.

1039	Surfaced on lifeguard station. The Japs jammed Okinawa badly last night. We have no dope on our cover as we could copy only that part of the message which concerned BATFISH.
1130	B-25 at five miles turned toward and challenged with lights; answered and called frantically on VHF.
1131	Five bombs, beautiful first order detonations, not too close on port beam. We dived - too late. No damage.

Small replied with the correct recognition signal and tried to contact the plane on the submarines radio, but for some reason, the B-25 made a bombing run and dropped five bombs of the submarines port beam. Fortunately, they all missed.[80] About a half hour after the attack, Small approached Bleicher and asked for information about their particular airplane:

> When all was clear, the captain asked me about our planes.
> He described the one that attacked us perfectly. It was one
> of our 820th B-25's. We had assumed, too early, that we
> were safe, after our rescue.[81]

Bleicher apparently knew who the pilot of the B-25 was as he was part of the bomb run against the railroad bridge and was on the right wing of flight leader Dan Hill. This pilot also had his B-25 shot up on the way out from the target area; however, he actually did make it all the way back to Okinawa. This same pilot had another mission three days later. Bleicher described it like this:

> As he was flying, his plane developed a fuel consumption
> problem. He was using too much fuel. He had nearly
> reached the point of no return, but the group had not yet

reached the intended target. Whatever the reason was, I never found out, but he did turn out of formation to return to Okinawa. He then came right on line with the Batfish sitting on the surface. As B-25 crewmembers, we had all been instructed not to attack any sub in this area because ninety-five percent or more were U.S. submarines. For whatever reason, probably the anxiety of losing credit for the mission, he popped open the bomb bay doors and dropped this bomb load near the Batfish.[82]

At 12:25 PM, *Batfish* surfaced. Fifteen minutes later, the SD radar picked up friendly planes at seven miles. Voices on the VHF indicated a "bogey" in the water with one of them saying "You drop; I'll spot for you." At 12:59 PM, the SD radar picked up a contact at five miles and closing fast and the contact was inside of one mile as *Batfish* slid under the surface of the ocean. Small decided to ride this raid out submerged even though they should have been on the surface as ComSubPac would probably send instructions on the treatment of the three aviators.

At 7:13 PM, *Batfish* surfaced into wind and mounting seas. At 10:20 PM, *Batfish* received a message telling *Blackfish* to take *Batfish's* lifeguard station as *Batfish* was to depart the area for Iwo Jima. On August 4, Mangeno, Bleicher and Van Epps departed *Batfish* for medical treatment at a hospital. Medical staff placed Mangeno's leg in a cast. Doctors stitched the gashes in Van Epps' leg and the surgeons praised the care received while on *Batfish* because there was no infection. Doctors also checked over Bleicher and he luckily only had a strained back.[83]

Towards the end of the war, with the increase in carrier activity and the increase in the number of submarines on patrol in the Pacific, the submarine's role had changed. Instead of targeting merchant shipping, they had more opportunities for warships, but also spent more of their time in lifeguard duty.[84] Twenty-two submarines were on Lifeguard stations on the last day of the war. Except for those in the Sea of Japan, which had run through the enemy mine fields in Tsushima Strait to cut the last remaining supply lines to the Empire, submarines had practically no duties other than lifeguard missions. Submarines had swept the seas clean, forming a tight blockading ring completely around the Empire. As the war ended, submarines metamorphosed from killers to lifesavers.[85] And this applied in particular to *Batfish*, which after sinking three Japanese submarines on its sixth patrol (and earning the name "submarine killer"), on the very next patrol, rescued three aviators and safely transported them back to Iwo Jima.

From its very inception, the Lifeguard League built a framework for cooperation between submarines and fighting aircraft. From the time regularly organized Lifeguarding began, until Lifeguarding ended, eighty-six submarines performed 504 rescues. A few submarines were lucky enough to bring in large numbers of flyboys, but the vast majority of them counted themselves fortunate to bring home one, two, or three zoomies. A remarkable and gratifying thing that came out of the Lifeguard League is the knowledge that most of the submariners who took part in rescues of aviators considered this duty, despite its obvious dangers, as a privilege and an honor. Many friendships, born of these meetings under desperate circumstances, between submarine sailors and zoomies have endured throughout their lifetimes.[86]

Chapter 7: Passing of the Torch

The war and *Batfish's* seventh patrol ended on the same day. *Batfish* departed its patrol area and head toward Guam with *Tigrone* (SS 419) slated to relieve *Batfish* on lifeguard station. The two subs were to rendezvous where *Batfish* would take on a P-51 aviator *Tigrone* rescued and *Batfish* would hand over their VHF unit to *Tigrone*, who was having great difficulty with theirs as outlined in *Tigrone's* patrol report:[1]

August 8

0925	VHF out of commission owing to cracked crystal for 140.58 megacycle channel
1418	Set course 150° T to head for U.S.S. BATFISH in order to rendezvous if possible and pick up spare crystal for 140.58 channel of VHF, if he has one.

August 9

0455	Exchanged recognition signals and calls over SJ radar with U.S.S. LIONFISH (SS 298)
0510	Sighted LIONFISH at 9,000 yards, closed to 200 yards to request loan of VHF crystal – No sale.

August 13

0714	We started one more thorough overhaul of the VHF.

1030	Found a broken ceramic part and pasted it together with glue. VHF receiver still no good
1455	Rescued P-51 aviator 4 miles off TENRYU KAWA LIGHT.
2230	Circling on station. Transmitted TIGRONE'S SECOND SERIAL to ComSubPac, reporting results and requesting early rendezvous to transfer aviator and pick up reliable VHF.

August 15

0100	Intercepted orders to BATFISH to proceed to GUAM for refit at end of today's strike. Here is where we get a VHF.
1425	Headed to seaward for rendezvous with homeward bound U.S.S. BATFISH to transfer survivor and pick up BATFISH VHF unit.
1808	Exchanged calls with U.S.S. BATFISH.
1827	Transferred pilot and received VHF unit from BATFISH

At midnight, *Batfish* crossed the eastern edge of its patrol area, on a direct route to Guam. The following day, August 16, found *Batfish* miles away from Japanese waters. Around 6 PM, *Batfish* received orders redirecting the submarine from Guam to Midway where on Wednesday, August 22 at 7:40 AM, *Batfish* moored in berth S-7. Ten minutes later the P-51 pilot departed, seasick but otherwise no worse for wear. At 1:45 PM, *Batfish* departed Midway and headed for Pearl Harbor. On August 26, *Batfish* exchanged calls with PC 486, the submarine's escort into Pearl Harbor where at 7:59 AM, *Batfish* moored port side to *Flying Fish* (SS 229), U.S. Submarine Base, Pearl Harbor.

On September 2, *Batfish* got underway at 9:50 AM in accordance with ComSubPac Operation order #192-A-45. The destination was Mare Island, California. Other submarines including *Tunny* (SS 282), *Pomfret* (SS 391) and *Spadefish* (SS 411) joined *Batfish* on the journey eastward. On Sunday, September 9, *Batfish* arrived at San Francisco and at 9:53 AM passed under the Golden Gate Bridge. A short time later, around 3:30 PM, the submarine reached its destination where it moored alongside Finger Pier 24 at Mare Island. On September 10, after unloading all ammunition and pyrotechnics, *Batfish* switched berths and at 4:06 PM, moored on the starboard side to the *Seahorse* (SS 304) at Pier 6, Navy Yard, Mare Island, where it began its "inactive overhaul", to prepare her for peacetime service.

On April 6, 1946, the Navy decommissioned *Batfish* from the Regular Navy and assigned the submarine to the Pacific Reserve Fleet as a training vessel. After six years of reserve duty, *Batfish* returned to active duty as the Korean War gained intensity. In January 1952, *Batfish* received her reactivation overhaul. On March 7, 1952, the Navy recommissioned *Batfish* with Lieutenant Commander Robert J. Jackson commanding.

After six weeks of readiness training, final corrective repairs, and loading of supplies, *Batfish* sailed for San Diego on March 28 to train and provision before continuing on to her new homeport in Key West, Florida. *Batfish* set course via the Panama Canal for Key West, arriving there May 9. As a unit of Submarine Division 122, U.S. Atlantic Fleet, she served the remainder of her commissioned career engaged in training operations in the Caribbean, the West Indies and along the eastern seaboard of the United States.

Deactivated for good on May 5, 1957, the Navy decommissioned *Batfish* on August 4, 1958 at the Charleston Naval Shipyard and assigned the submarine to the Charleston Group, U.S. Atlantic Reserve Fleet. In the summer of 1959, the Navy reassigned *Batfish* as a naval reserve training ship and transferred her to New Orleans. There, in 1962, the Navy reclassified *Batfish* as an auxiliary submarine (*AGSS 310*).

Batfish continued to serve at New Orleans and remained there until November 1, 1969 when the Navy struck her name from the Naval Vessel Registry. The Navy towed *Batfish* to the Naval Inactive Ship Facility, Orange, Texas, to await disposal. She was twenty-six years old. Obsolete, remembered by few and unknown to most, *Batfish's* hatches were sealed. Empty of submariners for the first time, her fate was uncertain and limited to three possibilities. The Navy could sell or give the submarine to a foreign country; the Navy could cut up the submarine for scrap; or the submarine could become a permanent war memorial as a few of her sisters had. Fortunately, *Batfish* was not given away or scrapped. The submarine's fate was to become a museum. In February 1972, the Navy transferred *Batfish* to the Oklahoma Maritime Advisory Board and tugs brought *Batfish* up the Arkansas River to Muskogee, Oklahoma. There, *Batfish* was placed in a dry berth and opened to the public as a memorial to Oklahoma combat submariners where she still servers today.

U.S.S. *Batfish* (SSN-681), a Sturgeon-class nuclear submarine, was the second ship of the United States Navy named for the batfish. Sturgeon-class submarines had a displacement of 3,860 tons surfaced and 4,630 tons submerged. The overall length was 292 feet, with a maximum width of 32 feet, a draft of 29 feet and a maximum speed 20+ knots. There were four twenty-one inch torpedo tubes that used the Mark-48 torpedo. A Sturgeon-class submarine had a complement of 107 personnel (12 officers and 95 enlisted).

The Electric Boat Division of General Dynamics Corporation laid down the SSN-681's keel on February 9, 1970 at Groton, Connecticut. The nuclear *Batfish* was launched on October 9, 1971, being sponsored by Mrs. Arthur R. Gralla, and was commissioned on September 1, 1972 with Commander Richard E. Enkeboll as the submarines first skipper. *Batfish* reported to her homeport, Charleston, S.C., on October 7, 1972 and then conducted shakedown operations in the West Indies through November. Next, weapons testing and inspections occupied the nuclear submarine during the first six months of 1973.

The SSN-681 performed many duties while in service including a supporting role in a major antisubmarine warfare operation with naval units from Turkey, Great Britain and Italy. It operated with British and Dutch air and surface forces and was involved in a location and recovery mission. *Batfish* regularly took part in large fleet exercises and conducted special operations in the Atlantic. Specific operations included the NATO exercises "Northern Merger", "Devil Foil", "Teamwork 76", "Dogfish" and a multi-environment, multi-threat exercise held in the Gulf of Mexico called "Gulfex 79".

Her most interesting special mission, one that brings back thoughts of her predecessor, the SS-310, was "Operation Evening Star". On March 2, 1978, the SSN-681, commanded by Commander Thomas Evans, left Charleston, South Carolina, on what would transpire to be a remarkable seventy-seven day patrol, ending on May 7.

On March 17, *Batfish* detected a Soviet Navy Navaga-class ballistic missile submarine (NATO reporting name "Yankee I") in the northern Norwegian Sea. The Soviet submarine was 200 miles above the Arctic Circle. The U.S. Navy believed the Soviet submarine was heading for America's East Coast and carried sixteen nuclear missiles. *Batfish* trailed the "Yankee" anywhere from 7,000 to 10,000 yards and collected valuable information on how the Soviets operated. During the next fifty days, the "Yankee" never detected *Batfish* and contact with the Soviet submarine was lost only twice: first during a bad storm and second when a fishing fleet passed overhead. Both times *Batfish* quickly reacquired the Soviet submarine as by then *Batfish* sonar knew the Soviet submarine's "acoustic signature" and could relocate the "Yankee" without too much trouble. *Batfish's* crew knew exactly where the Soviet submarine went as the mission tracked the Soviets' route and mapped the area the Soviets were patrolling.[2]

Batfish remained in service until November 2, 1998 when she was decommissioned. The Navy struck SSN-681 from the Naval Register on March 17, 1999 and disposed of by submarine recycling on November 22, 2002 through the Nuclear Powered Ship and Submarine Recycling Program at Puget Sound Naval Shipyard, Bremerton, WA.

Batfish and *Batfish*. One submarine remains, one does not. The World War II *Batfish* passed its namesake on to the nuclear *Batfish*. Both submarines encountered enemy submarines and both succeeded in their respective tasks. The nuclear *Batfish* did not share the same fate as the World War II *Batfish*. In essence, the 681 passed the torch back to the 310 so that people would not forget her service. Three crews in two submarines with one mission: to serve, to educate, to honor and to remember.

<u>Note</u>: much of the information regarding the decommissioning and re-commissioning was summarized from two very helpful websites:

- http://www.history.navy.mil/danfs/b3/batfish-i.htm (accessed 4-22-09)
- http://www.hnsa.org/ships/batfish.htm (accessed 4-22-09)

Information regarding the nuclear Batfish, SSN-681, in addition to the *Seattle Times* article, was summarized from this helpful website:

- http://www.navsource.org/archives/08/08681.htm (accessed 4-22-09)

Chapter 8: Lest We Forget

Batfish earned nine battle stars for her World War II service in the Pacific. All three skippers sank a combined sixteen ships and damaged three others during her seven war patrols. Over a period of four days in February 1945, Fyfe sank three Japanese submarines; a record not matched by any other U.S. submarine. For this feat, *Batfish* won the Presidential Unit Citation.

The Presidential Unit Citation was established by Executive Order on February 6, 1942. This was the nation's highest unit award, issued in the name of the President of the United States as public evidence of deserved honor and distinction to any organization, detachment, installation, ship, aircraft, or other unit for outstanding performance in action. The entire crew serving aboard the sixth war patrol was authorized to wear the Presidential Unit Citation that read as follows:

> "For extraordinary heroism in action against enemy Japanese combatant forces during the sixth War Patrol in the South China Sea from December 30, 1944 to March 3, 1945. Persistent and aggressive in her search for vital targets, the USS Batfish relentlessly tracked down the enemy and in three separate, brilliantly executed attacks, launched her torpedoes with devastating speed and skill and demolished three Japanese submarines. By the destruction of these formidable and threatening hostile Fleet units in a single War Patrol, the Batfish contributed significantly to the successful completion of the war. The courage, superb seamanship and gallant fighting spirit of

her officers and men reflect the highest credit upon herself and the United States Naval Services."

Individual awards included ten Bronze Star Medals, four Silver Star Medals, nine Battle Stars on the Asiatic- Pacific Area Service Medal and one Navy Cross. Most of these came on the sixth patrol including the Navy Cross to John K. Fyfe:

> The President of the United States takes pleasure in presenting the Navy Cross to John K. Fyfe, Commander, U.S. Navy, for gallantry and intrepidity and distinguished service in the line of his profession as Commanding Officer of the U.S.S. BATFISH (SS-310), on the SIXTH War Patrol of that submarine during the period 30 December 1944 to 3 March 1945, in enemy controlled waters at Luzon, in the Philippine Islands. Through his experience and sound judgment Commander Fyfe brought his ship safely back to port. His conduct throughout was an inspiration to his officers and men an in keeping with the highest traditions of the United States Naval Service.

The reader should take several key things away from this book. First, *Batfish* had brave, competent and capable officers and crew. The fact that Fyfe ended up with more kills had more to do with training, personal aggressiveness and a bit of luck. In addition, Fyfe was skipper for more patrols than Merrill and Small combined. Merrill got two ships, even though officially credited for only one. His second patrol was a combination of bad weather and bad luck. The results of the second patrol weighed heavily on him. You must remember that Merrill was "old school" and as such, trained differently than Fyfe. As for Small, by the time he made his first and only patrol in *Batfish*, the war was essentially over and Japanese shipping was virtually non-existent.

As for the tonnage issue, it is reasonable to think that the commanding officers would have no reason to lie about ships they sank. Granted, due to quick peaks through a periscope or black smudges on the horizon on a pitch-black night, positive ship identification was very difficult. After all, some ships looked very similar to each other and if the skipper could not plainly see the ship, then positive was almost impossible. For example, on the sixth patrol, Fyfe identified the three Japanese submarines as I-class submarines when in fact they were the much smaller RO-100 class submarines. It was a dark night by the crew's own admission. JANAC numbers are too low if not in tonnage than at least in the number of ships credited. Certain characteristics (loud explosions, screws stopping, breaking up noises, visually watching the ship sink) should count for something. It seems that if Japanese records did not support U.S. accounts, tonnages and sinking totals, the JANAC excluded these from the total count.

Speaking of the three Japanese submarines, one goal of this book was to outline the sixth patrol and understand how Fyfe performed the difficult procedure of sinking three Japanese submarines. Once details of the sixth patrol were established, Chapter 5 presented a resolution to the mystery around the identity of the first submarine Fyfe sank on February 10, 1945. All evidence points to the first submarine as an RO-class boat. As we have seen, Japanese leaders scheduled four RO-class Japanese submarines to make evacuation runs from northern Luzon. The *RO-46* actually made a successful, documented evacuation run. Fyfe definitely sank *RO-112* and *RO-113* on February 11 and February 13, respectively. Chapter 5 resolves two issues. First is that of misidentification. When Fyfe described the first submarine, he called it an I-class sub. Additionally, Fyfe initially identified *RO-112* and *RO-113* as I-class submarines. This seems to indicate that all three submarines were of the approximate same size and configuration. With the latter two actually RO-100 class subs, Fyfe misidentified the first submarine too and in reality, it was an RO-100 class boat.

The missing piece to the identification puzzle came in the way of a technical document called "Japanese Submarine and Shipborne Radar".[1] As outlined previously in Chapter 5, only three radar models were in use on Japanese surface ships and submarines at the end of the war, and Japanese submarines only used the Type 3 Mark 1 Model 3 as air-search radar. Additionally, only three classes of Japanese submarines had radar: the I-400 class, the I-10 class and the RO-100 class. This radar had a 150 megacycle with a pulse rate of 500 per second. All three Japanese submarines Fyfe sank were transmitting at 157-8 mgcs, 500 PRF. This means that the first submarine Fyfe sank was either an I-400 class, an I-10 class or an RO-100 class submarine. With the exception of *I-41* (erroneously attributed to *Batfish*), there are no reports of any I-class submarines being lost at the time or vicinity of the *Batfish* attack. Therefore, the first submarine was an RO-100 class submarine and definitely was not an RO-50 class submarine as that class did not have radar installed. This rules out *RO-55* as the first submarine, with credit now going to surface ships on February 7, 1945. All evidence points to the first submarine as *RO-115*.

A story so far untold at any great length is that of *Batfish's* lifeguard mission that resulted in the rescue of three downed aviators. Unfortunately, Mr. Nathan Mangeno and Mr. Robert Bleicher have passed away. Mr. James Van Epps was located and he was very gracious in providing all the information he had, including a personal narrative of the event. Mr. Bleicher's two articles were beneficial, telling the account from his viewpoint. The combined narratives from Bleicher and Van Epps along with the patrol report, gives a new perspective to the rescue. This story, an important part of the seventh patrol, needed telling and gives a true picture of how brothers-in-arms would give their all to help comrades in trouble. Even though the crew of *Batfish* may have thought they were just doing their job, from reading the accounts from the aviators, you can almost sense the relief they must have felt when they knew their rescue was certain.

Batfish arrived at the War Memorial Park in Muskogee, Oklahoma in 1972 and the museum had moderate success as a museum up until the late 1990's. At that point, two things happened to help change this. First, individuals organized different volunteer groups to help promote and restore the submarine; and second, the *Batfish* website launched. Volunteer groups active on the submarine include HAM radio operators, the Batfish Living History Association (re-enactors/education) and the Batfish Relief Crew (restoration). Muskogee features the Azalea Festival and the Five Civilized Tribes Museum with *Batfish* and War Memorial Park seemingly taking a back seat. The submarine's basic form of advertisement was an old dilapidated billboard that had one-third of the graphic missing. Getting the *Batfish* on the Internet gave it worldwide exposure from places like Japan, Russia, England, South America and of course various location across the United States. Because of this, visitor traffic has increased over the last few years.

Many people in Muskogee and the surrounding areas do not realize they have this treasure in their backyard. They do not realize the importance of what this submarine means and how fortunate they are to be so close to it. Unfortunately, this concept is lost on many individuals. Many stories, whether true or not, tell of theft and vandalism at the museum, and a visual inspection suggests these stories are more true than not. To think people would desecrate and disrespect a World War II memorial like that is truly sad. Fortunately, these aforementioned incidents are in the past and the best days for the museum are still ahead.

The goal of this book was to educate, entertain and reveal. *Batfish* served in World War II. *Batfish* trained in the 1950's. *Batfish* educates today. The museum at one time had a tape playing in the submarine while open for visitors. One statement on that tape said, "The *Batfish* was a real war hero in World War II." Reading the story of *Batfish*, one would have a hard time not agreeing with that statement. It did not sink the most ships; it did not make the most patrols or rescue the most downed aviators. However, *Batfish* still holds a record that will probably never be equaled… three enemy submarines in 76 hours. This amazing feat happened as Fyfe and *Batfish* prowled the waters of the Philippines while part of a three-submarine wolf pack labeled Joe's Jugheads. In terms of sinking Japanese submarines, *Batfish* became Leader of the Pack.

Author Biography

Mark W. Allen is the *Batfish* Historian and Volunteer Coordinator for the War Memorial Park museum in Muskogee, Oklahoma. He also created and maintains the submarine/museum website: www.ussbatfish.com. Mr. Allen is a member of the Society for Military History, the United States Naval Institute, and the American Association of State and Local History. He recently completed a Master's Degree in Military History with a World War II emphasis from the American Military University. His thesis examined Japanese and American submarine operations during the Battle of Midway. He and his wife currently live in Collinsville, Oklahoma.

Appendix 1

Appendix 1 is an excerpt from *Batfish's* sixth patrol, documenting the attack on the first of three Japanese submarines attacked and sunk.

2210	Radar signal on APR at 158 mgcs, 500 PRF.
2250	SJ contact bearing 240 True, 11,000 yards. Commenced tracking. Target tracked on course 310°, speed 12 knots so went to battle stations and commenced approach, broadcasting dope to other wolves in pack. Saturation signals on APR at 158 mgcs which increased in intensity as range decreased.
2331	Commenced firing tubes 1, 2, 3, and 4 on 130° starboard track gyros practically zero, range 1850 yards torpedoes set for six feet using a 2° divergent spread. All missed.
2339	(10s-40s) Four end of run explosions. Pulled out to 5,000 yards off target's track and commenced new end around while making reload. The night was very dark, no moon, partially overcast and target was not seen on first run but was believed to be a Japanese submarine. Decided to close to visual range for next attack and verify type of contact but tentatively set torpedo depths at 4 feet, 2 feet, 2 feet, and 0 feet
0001	With range to target 1020 yards a Japanese I-class submarine was clearly visible from bridge. We were in a beautiful position - 90 track zero gyros so at
0002	Commenced firing tubes forward. #1 was a hot run in the tube, #2 hit, and number three passed over spot where submarine sank. The hit was accompanied by a brilliant red explosion that lit up the whole sky and the target sank almost immediately Radar indications on the APR ceased abruptly. This radar signal was apparently non-directional type, and probably anti-aircraft since we closed to 900 yards without his giving any indication that he was aware of our presence. Target disappeared from visual sight and

on radar screen almost immediately, screws stopped and loud breaking up noises were heard on sound gear.

0010   Heard one end of run explosion.

0015   Commenced reload forward, sent results of attack to pack commander and rigged searchlight preparatory to returning to scene and search for survivors.

0120   Very strong oil smell, heavy slick on water. A cut shows we are two miles east of the point of attack. Turned on searchlight and after a short experiment decided we were advertising ourselves needlessly and accomplishing little except ruining the night vision of the bridge personnel and probably drawing airplanes.

Appendix 2

Appendix 2 is an excerpt from *Batfish's* sixth patrol, documenting the attack on the second of three Japanese submarines attacked and sunk.

1915	Radar signals on APR at 158 mgcs, 500 PRF. Since this is the same radar as we found on our submarine target last night, started searching very carefully on SJ and swung ship in order to find null in the signal, thereby determining the approximate true bearing of the source.
1951	Radar contact on SJ at 8,000 yards, bearing 310° True. Manned battle stations and commenced tracking. Since, if anything, it is darker than last night; and since we had found how ineffective the Jap radar was, decided to make a surface attack if possible and close target sufficiently to identify him by class.
2037	Sighted target from bridge at range 1,300 yards, identified as submarine with no shears, very low in water, and perhaps slightly smaller than our last target.
2043	With range to target 1,200 yards, on a course for a 90° starboard track, had made up my mind to shoot when the gyro angles decreased 10 more degrees to 10° left when at
2043	(30s) Signal on APR went off and target dove. Changed course to left and speeded up, in the meantime trying to reconcile myself to the fact that I had lost this one by trying to wait for the theoretically perfect set up. Why he dove became a point of discussion.
2105	Just one half hour later sound heard a swishing noise from general direction of target that was universally accepted as the sound of a submarine blowing his ballast tanks. At
2106	Sure enough, APR showed that 158 mgcs was back on and SJ made contact 8,650 yards, bearing 018° True. Whether the target head us or thought he heard us; saw us or thought he saw us; had us on his radar or thought he

did or just make a normal and routine night dive I don't know; but I do know that unless he has radar detector that will intercept our SJ, he's going to have a hard time finding us this time.

2109   Manned battle stations and started end around.

Appendix 3

Appendix 3 is an excerpt from *Batfish's* sixth patrol, documenting the attack on the third of three Japanese submarines attacked and sunk.

0155 Weak APR signal at 157 mgcs, 500 PRF. In hopes that this may be another Nip sub, started swinging ship to get approximate bearing of source.

0215 SJ radar contact 220° True, range 10,700 yards. Commenced tracking.

0227 Target tracks on base course 120° at 7 knots. Looks like another Nip sub so manned battle stations submerged and commenced approach.

0412 Dove on targets track at 6,800 yard range and went to radar depth.

0430 Swung for 90 track with stern tubes. Tide rips are making depth control and steering very difficult and I hope they don't adversely effect the torpedo.

0448 Commenced firing 3 tubes aft on an 80 starboard track, zero gyros 1500 yard torpedo run, using a 1 knot speed spread. Torpedoes set for 6 feet.

0449 (30s) Saw first torpedo hit and target sank immediately. Target could be seen blowing apart on radar screen and the explosion was accompanied by a large yellow ball of fire and seen through periscope. The second and third torpedoes missed, not due to errors in data, but because target sank so quickly.

Appendix 4

Appendix 4 is an excerpt from USS *Ulvert M. Moore* (DE 442) deck log, describing the depth charge attack of an unknown Japanese submarine on 31 January 1945.

2045	USS BELL (DD 587) reported sound contact; made depth charge attack.
2047	USS O'BANNON made depth charge attack.
2049	USS BELL reattacked with depth charges; reported large explosion and oil slick
2223	Contact regained.
2227	Fired full hedgehog pattern; three explosions in rapid succession heard on sonar gear and on fathometer.
2248	Regained contact.
2252	Fired full hedgehog pattern; a single explosion was hear on sound gear and in engine room.
2301	Regained contact.
2302	Fired full hedgehog pattern; sharp crack heard on sound gear followed by bubbling and hissing noises, heard on sound gear and by personnel on fantail.
2316	Regained contact.
2337	Fired full hedgehog pattern; two explosions heard on sound gear and in engine room.
0010	Regained contact.
0015	Fired hedgehogs. Three rapid violent explosions heard on sonar gear. Large explosion in water seen and heard by bridge personnel eighteen seconds after firing. Accompanying ships reported also hearing explosion.
0019	Tremendous explosion astern; jarred ship. Large area of exploding area and burning gasses sighted. All other ships reported hearing and seeing explosion.
0020	USS JENKINS reported large area troubled water and strong burnt-powder fumes, continuing search of area.

0050   USS JENKINS reported that no sonar contact had been obtained. This ship ordered in to search for debris.

0200   Ceased searching area after obtaining no further sonar contact and noting following evidence of a kill: Strong Diesel fumes from oil slick, man's jacket or life belt, planks and bits of wood, scraps and sheets of white paper. Ordered by O.T.C. to rejoin C.T.G. 77.4 in company with USS BELL; USS JENKINS and USS O'BANNON to search area until daylight. Submarine assessed as definite kill by O.T.C.

Appendix 5

Appendix 5 is an excerpt from *Archerfish's* sixth patrol, documenting the attack on the unidentified Japanese submarines attacked and sunk on 14 February 1945.

2008	SJ contact 030°T, 6,000 yards.
2010	A couple of erratic rapidly closing range gave appearance of another plane contact. Made quick dive.
2012	Sound picked up high speed screws. Tracked aft.
2031	Surfaced. Changed course to head for contact.
2053	Picked up contact on SJ at 7,200 yards. Continued to close at full speed. His speed 10½ knots.
2115	Range closed to 2,650 yards. Could see target as being low and probably a submarine. If not, a PC boat.
2117	All stop. Got a turn count of 256 rpm. Checked IFF and no response. No SJ interference. His course 235° with 25° zigs. Zigs are irregular in time.
2148	Sent message to Bennets Blazers reporting we had a contact with no radar interference and asked for their positions.
2145	Kept range between 5,000-6,000 yards while we worked up his starboard side. Waited for position reports from the Blazers, decoded all messages in to present time, rechecked all serial messages and zone notices as complete.
2309	Changed course to head in for attack. Before deciding to attack the following facts were carefully considered.

1. All friendly submarines were well clear. The BRILL about 200 miles west of us and all the Blazers reported positions about 140 miles east of us.
2. A screw count of 356 rpm for 10-11 knots indicates enemy. That turn count would give one of our boats a speed of about 18 knots.
3. No radar interference of any kind and no indications that we were detected as close as 2,650 yards.
4. No signals on sound.

5. No IFF response.

6. On a course heading to the northern tip of Luzon.

7. If the target was a PC, he was in a submarine patrol zone.

2315   By sight from the bridge the target was seen to be a submarine. The conning tower was more square than ours, no periscope shears, no gun platforms forward and aft of the bridge. Conning tower about half way between bow and stern. Deck flat.

2317   (10s) Fired #3 tube.

2317   (20s) Fired #4 tube.

2317   (30s) Fired #5 tube.

2317   (40s) Fired #6 tube.

No hits. A possible reason is that he zigged toward us and it was undetected. It was not possible to give angle on the bow. The track was less than was desired, but the range was closing quite rapidly and it was necessary to fire early to avoid detection. The torpedoes were set at 3 feet earlier due to the possibility of a PC boat and were not changed. The sea was calm and no reason to expect an erratic run. We swung left with full rudder and flank speed. Minimum range broadside 920 yards and details of silhouette checked with previous inspection.

2320   (15s) Due to wakeless torpedoes and apparently poor lookouts, he continued on. Fired #7 tube.

2320   (25s) Fired #8 tube.

2320   (35s) Fired #9 tube.

2320   (45s) Fired #10 tube.

2320   (45s) Hit. Probably first stern tube. The enemy sub was momentarily completely illuminated with the large white flash and again the features checked. Range about 2,000 yards. The radar pip started to disappear immediately and the target was no longer visible from the bridge. The pip disappeared completely about 1½ minutes after the hit and at 3,200 yards.

Glossary

Angle on the bow: The angle between the line of sight and the target's bow measured to port or starboard of the target's bow from 0 degrees to 180 degrees.

Approach Phase: The period during which the submarine maneuvers into position for commencing the Attack Phase.

Approach Course: The course or courses taken by the submarine during the Approach Phase.

Attack Phase: The period during which the submarine maneuvers for a firing position.

Distance to the Track: The perpendicular distance from the submarine to the target's track extended.

Divergent Spread: A spread in which the torpedoes of a salvo intersect the target's track at different points along the target's length and at different torpedo track angles.

Gyro Angle: The angle between the longitudinal axis of the submarine and the final torpedo track measured right or left of the bow or stern (bow for bow shots, stern for stern shots) of the submarine from 0 degrees to 180 degrees.

Normal Approach Course: The course which is equal to the true bearing of the target, plus or minus 90 degrees in the direction to close the target's track.

Salvo: A number of torpedoes fired at short-intervals at the same target.

Spread: A spread is a salvo of torpedoes fired to hit different points along the length of the target. A salvo of torpedoes is spread to cover errors in the estimates of enemy's course, speed, and range.

Spread Angle: The additional gyro angle, over that required for hitting the same point of a moving target, applied to successive torpedoes for producing the desired spread.

Torpedo Run: The total distance in yards traveled by the torpedo from the tube to the target.

Track Angle: The angle at the point of intercept between the target ships course and the submarine's course measured to port or starboard of the target ship's bow toward the submarine.

Torpedo Track Angle: The angle at the point of intercept between the target ships course and the reverse of the torpedo's course, measured to port or starboard of the target's bow.

Bibliography

Alden, John D. *The Fleet Submarine in the U.S. Navy: A Design and Construction History*. Annapolis, MD: Naval Institute Press, 1979.

———. U.S. *Submarine Attacks During World War 2*. Annapolis, MD: United States Naval Institute, 1989.

Andrade, Jr., Ernest. "Submarine Policy in the United States Navy, 1919-1941." *Military Affairs* 35, no. 2 (April 1971): 50-56.

Beach, Jr., Edward L. *Submarine!* Annapolis, MD: Naval Institute Press, 2003.

Benere, Daniel E. "A Critical Examination of the U.S. Navy's use of Unrestricted Submarine Warfare in the Pacific Theater During World War II." Newport, RI: Naval War College Joint Military Operations Department, May 1992.

Blair, Clay, Jr. *Silent Victory: The U.S. Submarine War Against Japan*. Philadelphia and New York: J. B. Lippincott Company, 1975.

Bleicher, Robert L. "Batfish Rescue." *Friends Journal*, Fall 1997, 27-32.

———. "A Day of Loss." *The Crow Flight*, June 2007, 10-11.

Boyd, Carl, and Akihiko Yoshida. *The Japanese Submarine Force and World War II*. Annapolis, MD: Naval Institute Press, 1995.

Carpenter, Dorr, and Norman Polmar. *Submarines of the Imperial Japanese Navy*. Annapolis, MD: Naval Institute Press, 1986.

Christly, Jim. *U.S. Submarines, 1941-45*. New York: Osprey Publishing, 2006.

Cope, Harley, and Walter Karig *Battle Submerged: Submarine Fighters of World War II*. New York: W.W. Norton & Company, Inc., 1951.

Dear, I. C. B., ed. *The Oxford Companion to World War II*. Oxford and New York: Oxford University Press, 1995.

DeRose, James F. *Unrestricted Warfare: How a New Breed of Officers Let the Submarine Force to Victory in World War II*. Edison, NJ: Castle Books, 2000.

Dictionary of American Naval Fighting Ships.1991. http://www.hazegray.org/danfs/submar/ss310.htm (Accessed 10 May 2009).

Enright, Joseph F. *USS Archerfish War Patrol Report 6*. College Park, MD: National Archives and Records Administration, 1945.

Friedman, Norman. *U.S. Submarines Through 1945: An Illustrated Design History*. Annapolis, MD: Naval Institute Press, 1995.

Fyfe, John K. *USS Batfish War Patrol Report 6*. College Park, MD: National Archives and Records Administration, 1945.

———. *Log Book of the U.S.S. Batfish (SS310), February 1, 1945 through February 28, 1945*. College Park, MD: National Archives and Records Administration, 1945.

Gruner, William P. *U.S. Pacific Submarines in World War II*. Sunnyvale, CA: Strategic Simulations, Inc., Publication year unknown.

Hackett, Bob, and Sander Kingsepp. "HIJMS Submarine I-41: Tabular Record of Movement." 27 October 2003. http://www.combinedfleet.com/I-41.htm. (Accessed 6 July 2008).

———. "HIJMS Submarine RO-45: Tabular Record of Movement." 24 July 2004. http://www.combinedfleet.com/RO-45.htm. (Accessed 6 July 2008).

———. "HIJMS Submarine RO-46: Tabular Record of Movement." 14 July 2007. http://www.combinedfleet.com/RO-46.htm. (Accessed 6 July 2008).

———. "HIJMS Submarine RO-55: Tabular Record of Movement." 16 October 2004. http://www.combinedfleet.com/RO-55.htm. (Accessed 6 July 2008).

———. "HIJMS Submarine RO-115: Tabular Record of Movement." 1 September 2005. http://www.combinedfleet.com/RO-115.htm. (Accessed 6 July 2008).

Hashimoto, Mochitsura. *Sunk: The Story of the Japanese Submarine Fleet, 1941-1945*. New York: Henry Holt and Company, 1954.

Haskew, Michael E. "World War II: November 1996 from the Editor." 19 August 1997. http://www.historynet.com/world-war-ii-november-1996-from-the-editor-2.htm. (Accessed 8 October 2008).

Helgason, Gudmundur "HMS Upholder: Submarine of the U Class." http://uboat.net/allies/warships/ship/3535.html (Accessed 11 May 2009).

"History: B-25 Mitchell Bomber." http://www.boeing.com/history/bna/b25.htm. (Accessed 04 May 2009).

Holmes, W. J. *Undersea Victory: The Influence of Submarine Operations on the War in the Pacific*. Garden City, New York: Doubleday and Company, 1966.

Hoyt, Edwin P. *Submarines at War: The History of the American Silent Service*. Briarcliff Manor, NY: Stein and Day, 1983.

Japanese Monograph No. 95. "Submarine Operations in the Philippines Area, September 1944 – March 1945. Washington, D.C.: Department of the Army, 1962.

Japanese Monograph No. 184. "Submarine Operations in Third Phase Operations Parts III, IV, and V Defense Operations, March 1944 0 August 1945. Washington, D.C.: Department of the Army, 1960.

Japanese Submarines and Shipborne Radar. San Francisco: U.S. Naval Technical Mission to Japan, 1945.

Jelinek, Pauline. "Voyage of the Batfish: 50 Days Tailing Soviet Sub." 2 March 2001. http://community.seattletimes.nwsource.com/archive/?date=20010302&slug=batfish02. (Accessed 22 April 2009).

The Joint Army-Navy Assessment Committee. "Japanese Naval and Merchant Shipping Losses During World War II by All Causes."

1947. http://www.ibiblio.org/hyperwar/Japan/IJN/JANAC-Losses/JANAC-Losses-6.html. (Accessed 8 May 2009).

———. "Japanese Naval and Merchant Shipping Losses During World War II by All Causes." 1947. http://www.ibiblio.org/hyperwar/Japan/IJN/JANAC-Losses/index.html#contents. (Access 9 May 2009).

Keith, Don. *In the Course of Duty: The Heroic Mission of the USS Batfish.* New York: NAL Caliber, 2005.

Kimmett, Larry, and Margaret Regis. *U.S. Submarines in World War II: An Illustrated History.* Seattle, WA: Navigator Publishing, 1996.

Kuenne, Robert E. *The Attack Submarine: A Study in Strategy.* New Haven, CT: Yale University Press, 1965.

Lockwood, Charles A. *Sink 'Em All: Submarine Warfare in the Pacific.* New York: E. P. Dutton & Co., Inc., 1951.

Lockwood, Charles A., and Hans Christian Adamson. *Zoomies, Subs and Zeros.* New York: Greenberg, 1956.

Lowder, Hughston E., and Jack Scott. *Batfish: The Champion "Submarine-Killer" Submarine of World War II.* Englewood Cliffs, NJ: Prentice-Hall, Inc., 1980.

Merrill, Wayne R. *USS Batfish War Patrol Report 1.* College Park, MD: National Archives and Records Administration, 1943.

Miller, Vernon J. *Japanese Submarine Losses to Allied Submarines in World War II.* Bennington, VT: Merriam Press, 1999.

Morrison, Samuel E. *The Liberation of the Philippines: Luzon, Mindanao, the Visayas, 1944-1945.* History of United States Naval Operations in World War II, Volume XIII. Boston, MA: Little, Brown and Company, 1984.

Orita, Zenji, and Joseph D. Harrington. *I-Boat Captain.* Canoga Park, CA: Major Books, 1976.

Padfield, Peter. *War Beneath the Sea: Submarine Conflict During World War II.* New York: John Wiley & Sons, Inc., 1995.

Poirier, Michel T. "Results of the American Pacific Submarine Campaign of World War II." 30 December 1999. http://www.navy.mil/navydata/cno/n87/history/pac-campaign.html. (Accessed 19 July 2008).

Rohwer, Jürgen. *Axis Submarine Successes of World War Two: German, Italian and Japanese Successes, 1939-1945*, Annapolis, MD: Naval Institute Press, 1999.

Roscoe, Theodore. *United States Submarine Operations in World War II*. Annapolis, MD: Naval Institute Press, 1949.

Santayana, George *The Life of Reason, Volume 1, 1905*. http://www.quotationspage.com/quote/2042.html. (Accessed 11 May 2009).

Schumacher, V. E. *USS Tigrone War Patrol Report 3*. College Park, MD: National Archives and Records Administration, 1945.

Small, Walter L. *USS Batfish War Patrol Report 7*. College Park, MD: National Archives and Records Administration, 1945.

Smith, Robert B. "The Triumph of USS Batfish." *WWII History*, March 2007, 72-77, 84.

Stern, Robert C. *The Hunter Hunted: Submarine Versus Submarine Encounters From World War I to the Present*. Annapolis, MD: Naval Institute Press, 2007.

Van Epps, James L., "Casualty Questionnaire." http://www.footnote.com/image/29038390. (Accessed 28 December 2008).

————. 2008, letter to author, 15 October 2008.

Walcott, William S., and W. H. Bell, Jr. *USS Ulvert M. Moore (DE442) Deck Log*. College Park, MD: National Archives and Records Administration, 1945.

Watts, A. J., and B. G. Gordon. *The Imperial Japanese Navy*. Garden City, NY: Doubleday & Company, Inc., 1971.

Wheeler, Keith. *War Under the Pacific*. Alexandria, VA: Time Life, Inc., 1998.

Whitman, Edward C. "Rising to Victory: The Pacific Submarine Strategy in World War II." Spring 2001. http://www.navy.mil/navydata/cno/n87/usw/issue_11/rising_victory.html. (Accessed 27 July 2008).

Zdon, Al., "Martin PBM Mariner." http://www.mnlegion.org/paper/html/christopher.html. (Accessed 30 April 2009).

Notes

Chapter 1: A Wolf in Sheep's Clothing

1. Hughston E. Lowder and Jack Scott, *Batfish: The Champion "Submarine-Killer" Submarine of World War II* (Englewood Cliffs, NJ: Prentice-Hall, Inc., 1980), 89-90.
2. Clay Blair Jr., *Silent Victory: The U.S. Submarine War Against Japan* (Philadelphia and New York: J. B. Lippincott Company, 1975), 808.
3. Robert E. Kuenne, *The Attack Submarine: A Study in Strategy.* (New Haven, CT: Yale University Press, 1965), 41.
4. Don Keith, *In the Course of Duty: The Heroic Mission of the USS Batfish* (New York: NAL Caliber, 2005), 5.
5. Charles A. Lockwood, *Sink 'Em All: Submarine Warfare in the Pacific* (New York: E. P. Dutton & Co., Inc., 1951), 289.
6. James F. DeRose, *Unrestricted Warfare: How a New Breed of Officers Let the Submarine Force to Victory in World War II* (Edison, NJ: Castle Books, 2000), 4.
7. Ibid.
8. Ibid.
9. Lowder and Scott, 89-90.
10. Ibid, 93.
11. Gudmundur Helgason "HMS Upholder: Submarine of the U Class." http://uboat.net/allies/warships/ship/3535.html (Accessed 11 May 2009).
12. George Santayana, *The Life of Reason, Volume 1, 1905.* http://www.quotationspage.com/quote/2042.html (accessed 11 May 2009).

Chapter 2: Commissioning and the Submarine War Against Japan

1. Dictionary of American Naval Fighting Ships, 1991, http://www.hazegray.org/danfs/submar/ss310.htm (accessed 10 May 2009)

2. Larry Kimmett and Margaret Regis, *U.S. Submarines in World War II: An Illustrated History* (Seattle, WA: Navigator Publishing, 1996), 9.

3. William P. Gruner, *U.S. Pacific Submarines in World War II* (Sunnyvale, CA: Strategic Simulations, Inc., Publication year unknown), 1.

4. Ibid., 2, 7.

5. Ibid., 6.

6. Ibid., 3, 11.

7. Michel T. Poirier, "Results of the American Pacific Submarine Campaign of World War II" (30 December 1999) http://www.navy.mil/navydata/cno/n87/history/pac-campaign.html. (accessed 19 July 2008).

8. John D. Alden, *The Fleet Submarine in the U.S. Navy: A Design and Construction History* (Annapolis, MD: Naval Institute Press, 1979), 101.

9. Norman Friedman, *U.S. Submarines Through 1945: An Illustrated Design History* (Annapolis, MD: Naval Institute Press, 1995), 209.

10. Jim Christly, *U.S. Submarines, 1941-45* (New York: Osprey Publishing, 2006), 17-21.

11. Ibid., 311.

12. Edward C. Whitman, "Rising to Victory: The Pacific Submarine Strategy in World War II" (Spring 2001) http://www.navy.mil/navydata/cno/n87/usw/issue_11/rising_victory.html. (accessed 27 July 2008).

Chapter 3: On the Hunt

1. The Joint Army-Navy Assessment Committee "Japanese Naval and Merchant Shipping Losses During World War II by All Causes." 1947. http://www.ibiblio.org/hyperwar/Japan/IJN/

JANAC-Losses/JANAC-Losses-6.html. (accessed 8 May 2009).

2. Wayne R. Merrill, *USS Batfish War Patrol Report 1* (College Park, MD: National Archives and Records Administration, 1943), 30.

3. The Joint Army-Navy Assessment Committee "Japanese Naval and Merchant Shipping Losses During World War II by All Causes." 1947. http://www.ibiblio.org/hyperwar/Japan/IJN/JANAC-Losses/index.html#contents (access 9 May 2009).

4. John D. Alden, *U.S. Submarine Attacks During World War 2* (Annapolis, MD: United States Naval Institute, 1989), 177.

5. Clay Blair Jr., *Silent Victory*, 505.; W. J. Holmes, *Undersea Victory: The Influence of Submarine Operations on the War in the Pacific* (Garden City, New York: Doubleday and Company, 1966), 288.

6. Alden, x – xi.

Chapter 4: The Hunter Hunted

1. I. C. B. Dear, ed. *The Oxford Companion to World War II* (Oxford and New York: Oxford University Press, 1995), 42.

2. Ibid.

3. Ibid.

4. Theodore Roscoe, *United States Submarine Operations in World War II* (Annapolis, MD: Naval Institute Press, 1949), 449.

5. John D. Alden, *U.S. Submarine Attacks During World War 2*, 3.

6. Robert C. Stern, *The Hunter Hunted: Submarine Versus Submarine Encounters From World War I to the Present* (Annapolis, MD: Naval Institute Press, 2007), 2.

7. Clay Blair, Jr., *Silent Victory*, 493-494.

8. Helgason, Gudmundur "HMS Upholder", (accessed 11 May 2009).

9. Dear, 42-43.

10. Edward L. Beach, Jr., *Submarine!* (Annapolis, MD: Naval Institute Press, 2003), 228.

11. Dorr Carpenter and Norman Polmar, *Submarines of the Imperial Japanese Navy* (Annapolis, MD: Naval Institute Press, 1986), 155.

12. Vernon J. Miller, *Japanese Submarine Losses to Allied Submarines in World War II* (Bennington, VT: Merriam Press, 1999), 4.
13. Carpenter and Polmer, 155.
14. Roscoe, 451.
15. Blair, 494.
16. Joseph F. Enright, *USS Archerfish War Patrol Report 6* (College Park, MD: National Archives and Records Administration, 1945), 14-15.
17. Ernest Andrade, Jr. "Submarine Policy in the United States Navy, 1919-1941," *Military Affairs*, 35, no. 2 (April 1971): 50
18. Ibid., 55.
19. Ibid.
20. Daniel E. Benere , "A Critical Examination of the U.S. Navy's use of Unrestricted Submarine Warfare in the Pacific Theater During World War II" (Newport, RI: Naval War College Joint Military Operations Department, May 1992), 5.
21. Roscoe, 231.
22. Ibid., 69.
23. Ibid., 170.
24. Ibid., 319-20.
25. Ibid. 227.
26. Ibid. 292.
27. Ibid., 69.
28. Ibid., 55.
29. Kuenne, 41.
30. Roscoe, 312-13.
31. Fyfe, *USS Batfish War Patrol Report 6*, 22-34.
32. John K. Fyfe, *Log Book of the U.S.S. Batfish (SS310), February 1, 1945 through February 28, 1945* (College Park, MD: National Archives and Records Administration, 1945), 85.

Chapter 5: Mistaken Identity

1. W. J. Holmes, *Undersea Victory*, 428.
2. Larry Kimmett and Margaret Regis, *U.S. Submarines in World War II*, 128.
3. Clay Blair Jr., *Silent Victory*, 807.
4. Holmes, 428.

5. Michael E. Haskew, "World War II: November 1996 from the Editor" (19 August 1997) http://www.historynet.com/world-war-ii-november-1996-from-the-editor-2.htm (accessed 8 October 2008).

6. Blair, 807; Holmes, 428.

7. Blair, 807.

8. Theodore Roscoe, *United States Submarine Operations in World War II*, 450.

9. John K. Fyfe, *USS Batfish War Patrol Report 6*, 24.

10. John D. Alden, *U.S. Submarine Attacks During World War 2*, 177.

11. Zenji Orita and Joseph D. Harrington, *I-Boat Captain* (Canoga Park, CA: Major Books, 1976), 266.

12. Kimmett and Regis, 128.

13. Hughston E. Lowder, *Batfish*, 202.

14. Keith,193.

15. Orita and Harrington, 266.

16. Japanese Monograph 95, 27; Japanese Monograph 184, 94.

17. Bob Hackett and Sander Kingsepp, "HIJMS Submarine RO-55: Tabular Record of Movement." (16 October 2004) http://www.combinedfleet.com/RO-55.htm (Accessed 6 July 2008).

18. Bob Hackett and Sander Kingsepp, "HIJMS Submarine RO-115: Tabular Record of Movement." (1 September 2005) http://www.combinedfleet.com/RO-115.htm (Accessed 6 July 2008).

19. Orita and Harrington, 266.

20. Mochitsura Hashimoto, *Sunk: The Story of the Japanese Submarine Fleet, 1941-1945* (New York: Henry Holt and Company, 1954), 163.

21. Carl Boyd and Akihiko Yoshida, *The Japanese Submarine Force and World War II* (Annapolis, MD: Naval Institute Press, 1995), 167.

22. Robert C. Stern, *The Hunter Hunted*, 222.

23. Peter Padfield, *War Beneath the Sea: Submarine Conflict During World War II* (New York: John Wiley & Sons, Inc., 1995), 466.

24. Fyfe, *USS Batfish War Patrol Report 6*, 10-11.

25. Ibid., 26.

26. Lowder, 165.

27. Fyfe, *USS Batfish War Patrol Report 6*, 26, 29.

28. Watts and Gordon, *The Imperial Japanese Navy*, 340-342.

29. Alden, *U.S. Submarine Attacks During World War 2*, 177.

30. Charles A. Lockwood, *Sink 'Em All*, 288.

31. Robert B. Smith, "The Triumph of USS Batfish." *WWII History*, March 2007, 76.

32. Bob Hackett and Sander Kingsepp, "HIJMS Submarine I-41: Tabular Record of Movement." (27 October 2003) http://www.combinedfleet.com/I-41.htm (Accessed 6 July 2008).

33. Kimmett and Regis, 128.

34. Bob Hackett and Sander Kingsepp, "HIJMS Submarine RO-45: Tabular Record of Movement." (24 July 2004) http://www.combinedfleet.com/RO-45.htm (Accessed 6 July 2008).

35. Bob Hackett and Sander Kingsepp, "HIJMS Submarine RO-46: Tabular Record of Movement." (14 July 2007) http://www.combinedfleet.com/RO-46.htm (Accessed 6 July 2008).

36. Holmes, 428.

37. Hackett and Kingsepp, "HIJMS Submarine RO-46".

38. Samuel E. Morison, *The Liberation of the Philippines: Luzon, Mindanao, the Visayas, 1944-1945*. History of United States Naval Operations in World War II, Volume XIII (Boston, MA: Little, Brown and Company, 1984), 278.

39. Jürgen Rohwer, *Axis Submarine Successes of World War Two: German, Italian and Japanese Successes, 1939-1945* (Annapolis, MD: Naval Institute Press, 1999), 288.

40. Holmes, 429.

41. Hackett and Kingsepp, "HIJMS Submarine RO-55".

42. Orita and Harrington, 266.

43. Morison, 279.

44. Boyd and Yoshida, 167.

45. Orita and Harrington, 266.

46. Boyd and Yoshida, 167.

47. Alden, *U.S. Submarine Attacks During World War 2*, 177.

48. Holmes, 428.

49. Hackett and Kingsepp, "HIJMS Submarine RO-115".

50. Morison, 279.

51. William S. Walcott and W. H. Bell, Jr., *USS Ulvert M. Moore (DE442) Deck Log*. (College Park, MD: National Archives and Records Administration, 1945), 97, 102.
52. Hackett and Kingsepp, "HIJMS Submarine RO-115".
53. Walcott and Bell, *Moore (DE442) Deck Log*.
54. Joseph F. Enright, *USS Archerfish War Patrol Report 6*, 14-15.
55. Watts and Gordon, *The Imperial Japanese Navy*, 340.
56. Hackett and Kingsepp, "HIJMS Submarine RO-115".
57. Japanese Monograph 148, 92.
58. Japanese Monograph 95, 27.
59. Ibid.
60. Japanese Submarines and Shipborne Radar. San Francisco: U.S. Naval Technical Mission to Japan, 1945, 1.
61. Ibid., 8.
62. Ibid., 20-21.
63. Carpenter and Polmar, *Submarines of the Imperial Japanese Navy*, 45.
64. Ibid., 57.
65. Rohwer, 287-289.

Chapter 6: Salvation

1. Charles A. Lockwood, *Sink 'Em All*, 299.
2. Harley Cope and Walter Karig. *Battle Submerged: Submarine Fighters of World War II* (New York: W.W. Norton & Company, Inc., 1951), 121.
3. Ibid., 123.
4. Don Keith, *In the Course of Duty*, 266.
5. Charles A. Lockwood and Hans Christian Adamson, *Zoomies, Subs and Zeros* (New York: Greenberg, 1956), xi.
6. Edwin P. Hoyt, Submarines *at War: The History of the American Silent Service* (Briarcliff Manor, NY: Stein and Day, 1983), 223.
7. Keith Wheeler, *War Under the Pacific* (Alexandria, VA: Time Life, Inc., 1998), 135.
8. Clay Blair Jr., *Silent Victory*, 479.
9. W. J. Holmes, *Undersea Victory*, 445.
10. Wheeler, 135.

11. Holmes, 251.

12. Kimmett and Regis, *U.S. Submarines in World War II*, 94.

13. Theodore Roscoe, *United States Submarine Operations in World War II*, 472.

14. Kimmett and Regis, 94.

15. Holmes, 444.

16. Kimmett and Regis, 94.

17. Walter L Small, *USS Batfish War Patrol Report 7* (College Park, MD: National Archives and Records Administration, 1945), 3. Note: *Batfish* actions and movement are taken directly from the patrol report and are not referenced except for direct quotes.

18. Ibid., 7.

19. James L. Van Epps, letter to author, 15 October 2008.

20. "History: B-25 Mitchell Bomber" http://www.boeing.com/history/bna/b25.htm (accessed 04 May 2009).

21. Van Epps to author.

22. Bleicher, Robert L. "Batfish Rescue." *Friends Journal*, Fall 1997, 27.

23. James L. Van Epps, "Casualty Questionnaire" http://www.footnote.com/image/29038390 (accessed 28 December 2008).

24. Robert L. Bleicher, "A Day of Loss." *The Crow Flight*, June 2007, 10.

25. Bleicher, "Batfish Rescue", 27.

26. Van Epps to author.

27. Van Epps, Casualty Questionnaire.

28. Ibid.

29. Van Epps to author.

30. Bleicher, "Batfish Rescue", 28.

31. Van Epps to author; Bleicher, "Batfish Rescue", 28.

32. Bleicher, "Batfish Rescue", 28.

33. Ibid.

34. Van Epps to author.

35. Bleicher, "Day of Loss", 10.

36. Bleicher, "Batfish Rescue", 28.

37. Bleicher, "Day of Loss", 10.

38. Ibid.

39. Van Epps to author.

40. Bleicher, "Batfish Rescue", 28.
41. Bleicher, "Day of Loss", 10.
42. Van Epps, Casualty Questionnaire.
43. Bleicher, "Batfish Rescue", 28.
44. Van Epps to author.
45. Bleicher, "Day of Loss", 10.
46. Ibid.
47. Van Epps to author.
48. Bleicher, "Day of Loss", 10.
49. Van Epps to author; Bleicher, "Day of Loss", 10.
50. Van Epps to author.
51. Bleicher, "Batfish Rescue", 29.
52. Al Zdon, "Martin PBM Mariner." http://www.mnlegion.org/paper/html/christopher.html (accessed 30 April 2009).
53. Bleicher, "Batfish Rescue", 29.
54. Van Epps to author.
55. Bleicher, "Batfish Rescue", 29.
56. Bleicher, "Day of Loss", 10; Bleicher, "Batfish Rescue", 29.
57. Van Epps to author.
58. Bleicher, "Batfish Rescue", 29.
59. Van Epps to author.
60. Bleicher, "Batfish Rescue", 29.
61. Ibid.
62. Van Epps to author.
63. Small, 26.
64. Lowder, *Batfish*, 90.
65. Van Epps to author; Bleicher, "Batfish Rescue", 29.
66. Bleicher, "Batfish Rescue", 30; Bleicher, "Day of Loss", 10; Van Epps to author.
67. Bleicher, "Batfish Rescue", 30.
68. Lowder, 191.
69. Bleicher, "Batfish Rescue", 30; Bleicher, "Day of Loss", 10.
70. Bleicher, "Batfish Rescue", 30.
71. Lowder, 191.
72. Bleicher, "Batfish Rescue", 30.
73. Van Epps to author.
74. Small, 12.
75. Bleicher, "Day of Loss", 10.
76. Lowder, 191.

77. Bleicher, "Batfish Rescue", 29.
78. Van Epps to author.
79. Blair, 843.
80. Ibid., 844.
81. Bleicher, "Day of Loss", 10.
82. Bleicher, "Batfish Rescue", 32.
83. Van Epps, letter to author.
84. Hoyt, 286.
85. Lockwood and Adamson, 293.
86. Ibid.

Chapter 7: Passing of the Torch

1. V. E. Schumacher, *USS Tigrone War Patrol Report 3* (College Park, MD: National Archives and Records Administration, 1945), 8-17.
2. Pauline Jelinek, "Voyage of the Batfish: 50 Days Tailing Soviet Sub." (2 March 2001) http://community.seattletimes. nwsource.com/archive/?date=20010302&slug=batfish02. (Accessed 22 April 2009).

Chapter 8: Lest We Forget

1. Japanese Submarines and Shipborne Radar, 20.

Index

Page numbers with "*ill*" after them indicates a table or drawing or illustration
Page numbers with "*n*" or "*nn*" in them indicates a reference to endnotes

---